A Natural History of Boston's North Shore

A Natural History

University Press of New England

Hanover and London

# of Boston's North Shore

Kristina Lindborg

Published by University Press of New England
One Court Street, Lebanon, NH 03766
www.upne.com

©2007 by University Press of New England
Printed in the United States of America
Illustrations by Kristina Lindborg
Cover and text design by Joyce C. Weston
5 4 3 2 1

Library of Congress Cataloging-in-Publication Data
Lindborg, Kristina.
    A natural history of Boston's north shore / Kristina Lindborg.
        p. cm.
    Includes bibliographical references and index.
    ISBN-13: 978–1–58465–578–7 (pbk. : alk. paper)
    ISBN-10: 1–58465–578–X (pbk. : alk. paper)
    1. Natural history—Massachusetts—North Shore (Coast) I. Title.
    QH105.M4L56 2007
    508.744′5—dc22
                                                                2007013713

To all those who make this corner of
Massachusetts the treasure that it is.
And for Bill, friend, companion, and fellow
adventurer and Benjamin and Chappell,
artists par excellence.

Contents

Acknowledgments

I've had a love affair with the North Shore since my first visit. My mother and I had moved back to Boston from southern California. My aunt, uncle, and cousin lived in Hamilton and my grandmother was taking me to visit them by train.

North Station, in fact, the whole west end of Boston looked very different then; this was before the Boston Redevelopment Authority (BRA) grabbed the city's character by the throat and squeezed until it was rendered colorless beyond recognition. The Madison Hotel, Boston Garden, Joe & Nemo's, and the West End Cinema were all cooking under the ear-splitting squeals of the elevated train that winded its noisy way from Charlestown to Roxbury. The train station smelled of greasy peanuts and hot coffee and the benches in the waiting area were big and brown and had high backs.

The conductor was enthralling, speaking in his auctioneer's patter to announce the stops we'd be making ("LynnSwampscottSalemBeverlyNorthbeverlyHamiltonWenhamand I-p-s-w-i-i-i-ch) and I steadied myself for take-off, sitting on my hard-sided blue suitcase in order to look out the window. I was three years old.

The landscape that swept by me through the smudged train window was at once serene and exhilarating. I saw for the first time, gently sloping hills, open meadows, fir trees, rocky ledges hugging the shore, the spare elegance of New England architecture, and snow. I knew I was home.

My claim on a full-time address in Essex County didn't happen right away. But the place nevertheless had a claim to my holidays, summer vacations, spare moments, and, unabashedly, my heart.

My gratitude to my Hamilton relatives, Ann and Harmon Hunt, is unbounded. And not just because they endured my unannounced visits, teenage dramas, and colorful friends, although they sure did all that and then some. It has more to do with setting standards by example, not just talk, that sort of thing.

My uncle, a true Maine Yankee right out of central casting, will always be my hero. He was critically wounded on a destroyer in the Pacific theater during World War II; one gnarly hand never did assume its normal appearance. Yet I saw him use those twisted fingers to maneuver the tiniest jewel mechanisms with a surgeon's skillful precision in his work as a master watchmaker. He also could be found clambering up the scaffolding of many a New England church tower to give an old clock a second life. And when he decided he'd had enough of New England winters and would take the family south, he didn't pick up the phone to call a travel agent, he got the plans to build a thirty-five-foot wooden ketch. In his backyard. From trees that he felled from his family's land—in way-up-there Maine.

That was the beginning of years of adventures, some that I had the privelege to share, of cruising in the balmy turquoise waters of the Bahamas, the Caribbean, and throughout the West Indies. Uncle Harmon later built another wooden boat—a fifty-five-foot double-ended three-masted Herreshoff schooner. Also in his backyard.

The message I got, not in words (Harmon didn't really like to talk that much), but from example, was: don't make excuses, just find a way to get the job done, and for heaven sake, don't whine. My aunt, unconditionally loving all the time despite many physical challenges, conveyed the same message albeit in a more demonstrative fashion. Although legally blind throughout her adult life, her spunk, independence, courage, and unselfishness continue to inspire and humble me.

It was during my Hamilton visits that I connected with my "big sister" Barbara Hearne and her endlessly patient, supportive, and loving family. Her mother, Terry's, first inkling as to what our relationship was to portend came about when she discovered us smoking cigarettes under the bulkhead in their cellar. I was twelve, Barb, fourteen. Our North Shore adventures each summer and on school vacations were always fraught with mischievous escapades but her relentlessly optimistic parents must have just known, or prayed, that somehow we'd turn out okay. We did. And we both stopped smoking.

My thanks, too, to other North Shore friends and their equally forgiving and indulgent families: Guy and all the Maxwell clan, Michael, Letty, and the insanely generous Ridinger family, and my friend of the late-night road adventures, Camilla and her gaggle of artsy Schades. You guys are all what makes a place more than just a meaningless assemblage of vistas.

And for specific gratitude in the putting together of this book, I'd like to thank the following people who directly or obliquely helped it to come to fruition.

Thank you to Robert N. Oldale, author and emeritus geologist with the United States Geological Survey in Woods Hole for his patient and instructive explanations of the mysterious workings of the Earth's constant rumblings and shuffles. And while we're at it, to the entire Woods Hole scientific community. Our years living in that quirky village were invaluable for honing my skills as a reporter and clarifying the idea that we are all world citizens in the domain of scientific discovery.

Many thanks to Donald Slater, educator and assistant collections manager, and Bonnie Sousa, senior collection manager and registrar, both of the Robert S. Peabody Museum of Archaeology in Andover: their knowledge and enthusiasm for the exceptional Bull Brook artifacts they showed me was a boon and an inspiration. It helped the chapter write itself. Thanks to Dennis Larson, education coordinator at the Massachusetts Audubon Joppa Flats Education Center in Newburyport for taking the time to talk about the vast subject of migrating birds. Thanks to Arthur "Sooky" Sawyer, vice president of the Massachusetts Lobster-fishermen's Association in Gloucester for his help with sorting out the lobster numbers. An enormous thank you to the gracious librarians at the Ipswich and Hamilton-Wenham public libraries—I promise to get all the books back—and to the librarian at the Peabody Institute of Danvers for his nuggets about Folly Hill. Another nod to Boston's Museum of Science Library for their very helpful tracts on the Bull Brook excavation.

Thank you to the unnamed woman who stood up at the end of a lecture my husband was giving to ask when he would write another natural history book about the area that kids would understand. He declined. I didn't. Madam, I hope this does it for you.

Thanks to Michael McGrath, fellow Montserrat alum, for the use of her barn (and at a very good rate) to write the proposal for this book. Much gratitude to Montserrat College of Art for showing me early on that true artistic freedom comes with inspiration tempered by disciplined technique. And to the *Christian Science Monitor* for teaching me how to recognize and tell the story behind the story. My sincere thanks to

Jane D-S., Margit H., Lois C., Michael P., Roni R., and Richard H. for letting their light shine so brightly that I couldn't help but remember what I almost forgot. Thank you all again.

Thank you to my father-in-law, former Massachusetts governor, Frank Sargent, for his style, wit, and passion for making sure that future generations would be able to enjoy the pristine beauty of places like Essex County. Pup, as he was known in the family, was coming up with environmental initiatives in the State House way before it became fashionable or politically expedient to do so, especially for a Republican. When he was State Commissioner of Natural Resources, he and a few other like-minded visionaries drew up the legislation that established the Cape Cod National Seashore, a federal designation that protects the natural resources of nearly the entire coastline of the Outer Cape. And during his tenure as governor, he was responsible for a number of progressive environmental policies that continue to affect the marshes, woods, and rivers he loved so much. His expansive good will is sadly missed.

Thanks too, to former U.S. Congressman Gerry Studds, another far-sighted politician who stayed true to his mission of safeguarding the environment. During his lengthy stint in Washington, the Democratic Studds was focused and indefatigable in his efforts to protect U.S. fishing interests and the waters off the Massachusetts coastline. It was through his labors and hence his namesake that the Gerry E. Studds Stell-wagen Bank National Marine Sanctuary came into being, protecting the fish, whales, dolphins, and seabed from overfishing, pollution, and oil drilling. Studds was also a radio reporter's dream interview—he delivered intelligent, succinct sound bites in a voice right out of broadcasting school. He, too, is sadly missed.

And speaking of visionary, I'm so very grateful to my editor, Phyllis Deutsch at UPNE, for recognizing the niche this book could fill and for providing the follow-through to make sure it would happen. You reawakened my love of research and storytelling and I'm forever indebted. Thank you again.

Thank you to my parents, Laura and Oscar, for their love of the written word and shared artistic sensibilities. And to my grandmothers, Carmina and Edna, for their stories and memories of golden wheat fields in Italy and flower-laden meadows in upstate New York.

Thank you a gazillion times to my daughter, Chappell, for her innate sense of grace, beauty, and correct grammar. And to my step-son, Benjamin, for being a little boy (a long time ago) and teaching me how to fish for flounder.

Ah, and then there's Bill. I was news director of a funky mid-sized radio station on Bog Hollow Road in East Orleans when newly dating my husband, Bill. He came to see me at the station one day wearing a red chamois shirt, sleeves rolled to the elbow, khaki trousers, rolled up to the knees, and bare feet. He was tanned (he's always tanned, like George Hamilton, it's kinda spooky) and smelled of salty marshes and wood smoke. That was it. I knew I'd love him forever. I think Bill's feeling for, no, feeling *with* all things natural and living is as much a part of him as his eye color or his fingerprints. One can't be with him and not find wonder in the veined petals of a wildflower or beauty in the ungainly, helmet-shelled, spiky-tailed horseshoe crab. He'll rescue plants (often to my great dismay—poinsettias after Christmas are, well, pointless) that look like they've breathed their last and tenderly nurse them back to a healthy green existence. He'll transport spiders that have mistakenly crept into my daughter's field of vision to some safe place outdoors, away from the shrieks of human harassment. Each season holds delicious surprises and delights for Bill, possibilities abound. He'd probably say that I knew nothing about nature before I met him. But that's not true. I only knew next to nothing. But then, it's not necessarily the knowing of something but the loving of it that keeps it going, and that's where I must truly thank my husband for being the greatest mentor. So, I've tried my hand at seeing the seasons with a reporter's curiosity and a naturalist's love of what each tilt of the Earth reveals.

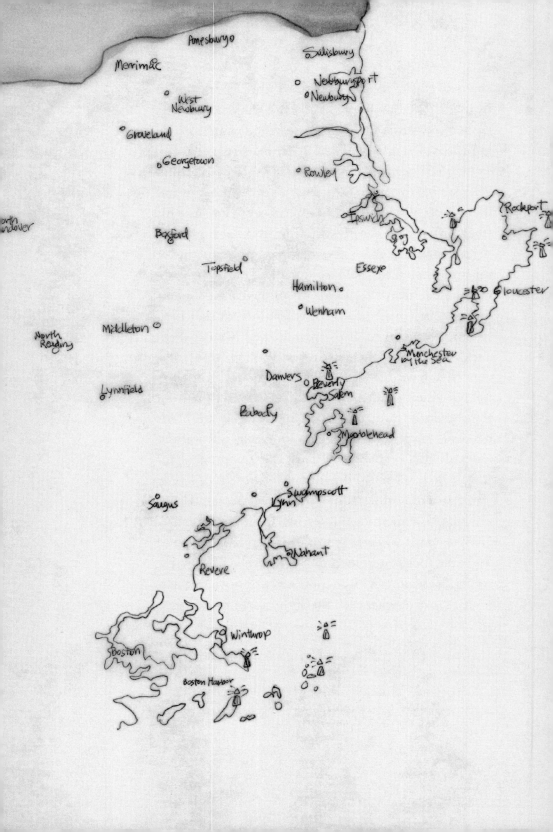

Rockport

"Nice day, huh, Brenda?" The grinning man in the drenched anorak shoots his question across the restaurant counter as he shakes the rain from his sleeves. The waitress considers a clever return, but instead just smiles and wearily nods in agreement. It's that kind of day here in Rockport. Last day of January. Cold, wet, relentlessly grey, and a nor'easter is bearing down hard on this stubby thumb of rocky shoreline known as Cape Ann.

From my vantage point in this landmark eatery, I can see sizzling white caps and bulging ocean swells easily four feet high—less than twenty feet offshore. Yet, here inside, thankfully, all is warm, dry, and calm. It's a study in contrasts that speaks for the nature of this Massachusetts region itself, from the cracked slabs of the granite headlands to the gently sloping drumlins, tidal creeks, expanse of salt marshes and all the way out into the deep, grey-green Atlantic. It's a natural-history haven and home to migrating birds, North America's largest marsh-dwelling mammal, a two-hundred-million-year-old living fossil, hump-back whales, and thousands of Paleoindian artifacts. And that's just the beginning of the list.

All this within an hour's drive of Boston (unlike its more illustrious cousin, Cape Cod)—and you don't even have to cross a bridge.

A Natural History
of Boston's North Shore

Chapter 1

A Rocky Beginning

Before there was Rockport, or any kind of port for that matter, there was the gathering of molten magma and interstellar dust here on Earth that formed the continent of Rodinia. Rodinia is one of three hypothetical supercontinents that geologists identify as having left their collective imprimatur on Massachusetts; the other two, Laurentia and Pangaea, were formed at a later time from the matrix of Rodinia. But more about that later.

Current estimates as to the Earth's age put it at roughly 4.6 billion years. Geologists figure that about one billion years ago, cratons, or the granite nuclei of continents, started bumping and crashing into each other. This restless activity on earth's rocky outer crust is known as plate tectonics. Stated simply, plate tectonics reveals that instead of being a solid shell, the Earth's surface is made up of enormous slabs, or plates, some up to sixty miles thick, which are drifting on top of the planet's soft underlying mantle—think saltine crackers floating on a rich clam chowder.

These rocky plates are adrift all over the Earth, and

they busily move both up and down and from side to side. This ongoing shifting, folding, churning, and grinding explains such geophysical phenomena as earthquakes, volcanoes, and tsunamis.

It also led to the formation of the supercontinent Rodinia about 750 million years ago. But not for long. A couple million years later, more plate movement broke up Rodinia. One chunk, known as the Laurentian craton, in time became the nub of North America; other bits split from Rodinia, migrated far south, and formed the supercontinent Gondwana. All that shifting and jostling of land masses eventually led to the formation of South America, Africa, India, Antarctica, and Australia.

Meanwhile, lots of things had been going on back up in Laurentia since it had parted company from Rodinia. Several volcanic island chains and at least two microcontinents smacked into and glommed onto eastern Laurentia's margin. Geologists figure that several suspect terranes that comprise the eastern half of Massachusetts were most likely rock formations from microcontinents

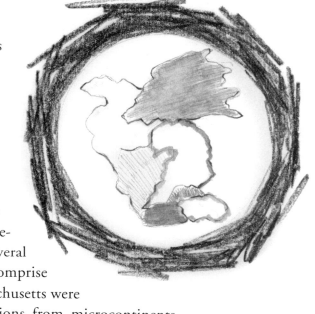

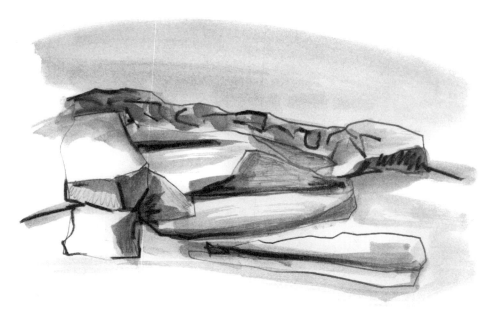

that chipped off Gondwana and smashed into each other while making their way to Laurentia some four to five hundred million years ago. Indeed, Massachusetts has lots of these chunks, plutons, of igneous or volcanic rocks that tell the action-packed story of Earth's churning, belching, smashing, and breaking activity of continent making and remaking.

So, here's what we've got so far. The Earth is not a solid shell, but rather a conglomeration of constantly shifting plates of rock drifting atop its soft interior mantle. About a billion years ago, the supercontinent of Rodinia was formed from smaller chunks or cratons. It broke up. What's left of it became Laurentia, which further crumbled to send chunks to the southern hemisphere. These pieces in turn regrouped to form the other supercontinent, Gondwana. Meanwhile, after more colliding, tearing apart, and crashing into each other, Gondwana and Laurentia met up again like estranged lovers to form that third supercontinent, Pangaea, which was finally all neatly assembled, well, sort of, about 245 million years ago.

But as we all know, there is no modern continent called Pangaea. Roughly two hundred million years ago, Pangaea began its restless rift apart, which resulted in the modern continents of North America and Europe, in addition to the beginnings of the Atlantic Ocean.

Clearly, when looking at the Earth's topography, one sees a planet that's a very active work in progress, and definitely not a static ball plodding through space. It also explains the fantastic diversity of landscapes that pop up in places like Cape Ann, the Merrimac Valley, and Plum Island.

Chapter 2

Ice

*I*n 1975, a Cape Ann fisherman was trawling his nets through waters about 180 feet deep, some eighteen miles north of Boston, not far from his homeport of Marblehead. His catch that day was . . . unusual.

Jumbled up within the tangled mass of kelp, flounder, and Jonah crabs, a hard and distinctly ridged object about six inches long glistened through the silt as he sorted his haul. It was a tooth, but the tooth of neither shark, whale, cod, nor any other marine animal for that matter. It was the tooth of a decidedly land-based mammal that lumbered heavily over the Massachusetts landscape some twelve thousand years ago. It belonged to a wooly mammoth. But there's more to the story. Some five years later, another Cape Ann fisherman, this time out of Swampscott, found a mastodon tooth less than six miles from where the mammoth tooth had been dredged.

What's significant about these finds is how handily they weave together so many stories; land and beach

formation, sea-level rise, the interplay of climate and ecosystems, and human migration patterns, to list a few. And if there were one word that joins these stories together seamlessly, it would have to be—glaciation.

Geologists say that there have been at least four major ice ages spanning the Earth's dynamic past. The most recent glaciation started about three million years ago in parts of Canada, northern Europe, and Asia. It occurred, as glaciers do, when the amount of yearly snowfall exceeded its melting. When that happened, underlying layers of snow crystallized into ice from the pressure exerted by top layers. When the ice sheet thickened to a depth of several hundred feet, the weight caused the bottom ice to become plastic and creep outward from the heavy center to its leading edges. About twenty-five thousand years ago, that ice sheet advanced from the Laurentian region of Canada and made its way south, doing what glaciers do best. It greedily scooped, scoured, pushed, and dragged everything in its path.

The glacier then spread out like cake batter in slow-mo at a rate of a few inches to a few feet per year. It even made its own weather pattern. The more the ice grew and covered the Earth's surface, the greater the amount of the Sun's energy that was reflected back into space. At one time, most of New England was buried under an ice sheet up to two miles thick.

But glaciers aren't forever. Roughly every twenty-five to fifty thousand years, warm weather patterns caused the glacial process to reverse itself. During these interglacial periods, the ice melted, beginning at the outer edges of the sheet. As it melted, the glacier left a heaping trail of wild debris in its wake. That's what happened in the northeastern United States about thirteen thousand years ago when the Laurentide ice sheet began its retreating meltdown.

This glacial debris, called till, is made up of rocks, sand, boulders, gravel, silt, clay—just about all the

stuff you see on the ground across New England and the Northeast region, sometimes in the most unlikely settings. Like a boulder the size of a two-car garage commanding someone's front lawn in Gloucester.

While the stubborn ice slowly yielded its frozen grip on the region, it resolutely shaped and contoured the distinctive features that we recognize today: geological characteristics such as the long, sloping hills called drumlins that tumble across the vast Ipswich marshes; kettle hole ponds that dot the Wenham landscape, and the

improbable boulder fields strewn about Gloucester's Dogtown Common. They're all a result of the Laurentide ice sheet, as are the great southern moraine land formations of Cape Cod, Nantucket, and Martha's Vineyard.

And of course, there are the beaches. Twenty thousand years ago when the glacial ice sheets were at their peak, global sea levels were about three hundred feet below what they are now. That's because so much of Earth's water was covering the surface as ice. So the coastline of New England—in fact, the entire East Coast—looked very different from what we see today.

For example, much of New England's Atlantic Continental Shelf, including parts of Georges and

Stellwagen Banks, was exposed, extending the coastline more than seventy-five miles beyond its current site. And as the climate warmed and the ice retreated, the once-frozen ground gave way to a rich carpet of tundra vegetation. This included plants such as grasses, mosses, lichens, and sedges—a tasty selection for grazing animals such as the wooly mammoth.

So, maybe it happened this way.

It's late winter. The weather is harsh and the ground is scoured. A lone, hulking mammoth is poking about the desolate landscape searching for some scrap of plant life before the long nightfall. He reaches a small patch of fluttering brown sedges and lowers his massive head. But in a blinding flash, he falls hard on his side and suddenly a long stick is jutting out from his heaving chest. The stick, a spear aimed with deadly precision, belongs to the hunter now emerging from his hidden post behind a boulder. He's not alone. The mammoth struggles to get up, but it's no use. More spears follow the first, leaving no question about what's to come next.

The hunters, a band of a dozen Paleoindian men and older boys dressed in rude patches of animal skins, move in for the kill. They will carefully carve up their prize, leaving its skeleton to the caprice of rain and rushing rivers. It will be carried out to the exposed shelf and, in time, silently disappear under the choppy surf and thick mud.

Chapter 3

Bull Brook

Aside from the mounds of dirt and gravel three stories high, dinosaur-like steam shovels, backhoes, and yawning cranes, there's not much to distinguish Bull Brook today. But toward the end of the last ice age, it sure must have been a happening place.

This Paleoindian site, discovered in 1949 by a group of dedicated amateur archaeologists, is to date the largest such site uncovered in New England and maybe the entire North America.

Exactly how and when these Paleo people came to the Cape Ann region or to North America, for that matter, is still a matter of debate and a "touchy subject" according to one archaeologist. But at least a few themes remain constant.

Paleo, or ancient, humans probably came in successive migrations to North America from northeastern Asia during the Pleistocene epoch, anywhere from twenty to thirty thousand years ago. During that time and extending to about ten thousand years ago, a land

bridge known as Berengia spanned some fifteen hundred miles, connecting the Asian and North American continents. As ice sheets began to retreat, hunters followed migrating herds of animals, perhaps caribou, into North America. The tundra landscape at that time flourished with grazing game such as mammoth, mastodon, bison, horses, and even camels.

Some migrating Paleos in canoe-like boats may have gone on to South America using an open route down the Pacific coast, while others may have pushed their way east using the ice-free corridors that sliced through the continental interior.

Unlike the arid Southwest, New England's cool, damp climate and acidic soil aren't well suited to preserving human artifacts. For that reason, much of what's known about Cape Ann's Paleo inhabitants has to be surmised from their stone tools. And the Bull Brook site is a virtual mother lode of tools.

Although final radiocarbon dating has yet to settle all the arguments, the date that archaeologists currently fix on Bull Brook is 12,640 B.P. (before the present). The picture that emerges from the site's age and size reveals a people and culture both resourceful and complex.

Bull Rock

The site was made up of forty-two campsites set in a large circle about five-hundred feet across. If each campsite housed an extended family of five to eight people, then more than three hundred people could have gathered there at the same time. Hunters may have used the site as a base camp during seasonal hunting migrations and bands may have convened to mark significant social events such as marriages and to exchange goods as a way to reinforce peaceful relations.

The type of stone tools they made also testifies to the ingenuity of these early American people. Thousands of stone artifacts, including the distinctive North American fluted or Clovis spearhead, scrapers for processing animal hide, and sinkers for fishing in nearby waters were all unearthed at the Bull Brook site before bulldozers set to their demolition task in 1960, turning what was arguably the Paleo find of the century into a sand and gravel pit.

These ancient toolmakers used antlers and hammer stones to do the chipping. Few if any of the Bull Brook stone tools were made from local materials. Most were made of Munsunun chert from northern Maine, many others of stone from parts of New York, New Hampshire, and Vermont. The hunters would carry the unfinished stone to Bull Brook and make their tools as they were needed. Sometimes they traded for the better grade rock.

But did these hunting groups meet every few years or more often? Could they have used astronomical

events as their guidelines? Did the diverse bands share a common language, culture, and belief system? These questions, as well as the bigger puzzle of what became of Paleoindian societies, don't lend themselves to easy answers. Some archaeologists think that as the climate warmed and the vegetation changed from tundra to woodlands, hunters may have followed grazing herds of game northward, eventually settling in the Canadian Arctic, becoming the people we now know as Inuit. Others speculate that they may have dispersed gradually throughout the region, becoming the Native American tribes that thrived before the arrival of European colonists.

Driving past the dusty heaps of sand, stone, and gravel that blanket the Bull Brook site, one can't help but wonder if the answers are still there, buried under the monuments to free enterprise.

Chapter 4

Early Spring
Chebacco Road, Hamilton

*T*he bleak days of February have reluctantly let go of their dreary hold. By the second week of March, the daylight has lengthened by four hours since the first of the year, and daytime temperatures are at times warm enough to make the damp soil smell like the promise of summer. By the side of the road in what easily could be mistaken for a tire rut or muddy puddle left by winter's melted snow, a vernal pool buzzes and hums with a riotous concerto of nascent life forms.

This seasonal habitat is both breeding ground and nursery to a host of amphibians, invertebrates, plants, and visiting waterfowl. The best time to crash their uninhibited scene is at night.

On this warm March evening, the frenzied whistles of the spring peepers are the first sounds to greet the ear. These Lilliputian frogs, no bigger than your thumbnail, are one of the earliest audible signs of spring's arrival. All winter long, these tiny denizens

have been snoozing away in hibernation under tree bark or clumps of earth waiting for clues of temperature, light, and moisture to wake them so they can get on with their noisy courtship.

The males produce the loud "peep-peep" to attract the females. They will then cling to them and fertilize the eggs that the females deposit in the murky waters of the pool.

Wood frogs add to the din with their "quack" calls, leaving their slimy egg masses like gelatinous alien blobs to hatch on the water's warm, scummy surface.

Vernal pools also play a key role in the life cycle of the spotted salamanders. These yellow-splashed, stout amphibians spend most of their adult lives,

which can extend for more
than twenty years, under-
ground. But they start out
here in these ephemeral pools.

Each spring, usually on
the first rainy night in March
warmer than 45 degrees Fahren-
heit, dozens of spotted salamanders
will head simultaneously for their vernal pool breeding grounds—often migrating back to the same pool where they
were hatched. The males gather in groups and
perform elegant courtship dances to attract the females. After the males leave spermataphores, small
jelly-like sacs of sperm, sticking to the leaf litter on the
bottom of the pool, the females take over. They pick
up the spermataphores and fertilize their eggs inter-
nally for about a week, then deposit up to three hundred eggs on any bits of twig, leaf, or pebble
submerged in the pool.

The larvae that hatch must find food and avoid
predators to ensure their survival to young adulthood.
And they have to do it before the pool
dries up by summer's end.
Once they metamorphose
by growing limbs and
lungs and losing fins and
gills, the salamanders can

crawl out of the pool and not return to it until they reach maturity a few years later. That's when the cycle will begin all over again.

A few miles west in the nearby woods and meadows of Appleton Farms, the American woodcock has returned from his winter migration to lure a mate with his wildly acrobatic courtship dance and distinctive calls of "Peent! Peent!" Killdeer also have returned to stake their nesting claims in the open fields. To the east, in the offshore waters of Gloucester, Atlantic white-sided dolphins gather in huge schools to play in the warming waters of March.

Chapter 5

Late Spring

Essex

I t's a warm spring morning on the Essex Marsh. The sky is an electric blue and new shoots of bright green grass are poking up through the soggy mud.

From a distance, it looks as if someone left a brown jacket in the middle of the otherwise empty marsh. It's balled up in these swaying ribbons of grass, not far from where the incoming tide is making little swirling pools of seawater. But it's not a jacket at all. It's a newborn deer. The fawn is cradled in the upright grasses, laying very still, its neck outstretched and ears alert, waiting for its mother's return.

This white-tailed deer is less than a week old. Its soft coat is reddish brown with rows of white spots splashed along its coppery back and sides. The color and pattern combination helps to camouflage the fawn from the predators, such as coyotes, who hunt and stalk the marsh. The spots will fade by the time the fawn is three to four months old. In addition to the

deer's keen sense of hearing, smell, and sight, its markings provide the fawn with an added survival feature.

The fawn's mother has cached, or intentionally left, the baby within earshot while she grazes on grasses and buds in another part of the salt marsh field. Since the fawn is odorless for the first four days of its life, the mother stays away from it until feeding time. This helps to protect the fawn from predators who could pick up the mother's scent. She'll come back to nurse the fawn at least eight times during the day, but for now, the best thing the young deer can do to protect itself is just to stay very still. After all, other than people and their dogs taking walks across the marshy fields, most of the predatory animals are nocturnal hunters. In the middle of the day, if the fawn doesn't move, it's

not likely to be seen. If the fawn should try to wander off, the mother can track it by means of a scent that the fawn secretes from glands between its hooves.

The white-tailed deer is the largest animal found on the marsh. It is a ruminant and like cows has four stomachs. The first stomach breaks down plant tissue while the other three help complete the digestion process. Ruminants eat first and chew later. This system lets the deer eat a lot of food quickly and then take cover from predators. It grazes on twigs, bark, spring grasses, sedges, and ferns around the borders of the marsh, and also will venture into residential backyards and gardens.

White-tailed deer are a controversial species in many of their habitats across the United States and especially here on the North Shore of Massachusetts. They are considered a "keystone" herbivore, or plant eater, because their eating habits have such a pronounced impact on many other plant and animal species.

Before European colonists settled here centuries ago, the deer population was kept in check by predators such as wolves and mountain lions. Now, besides human hunters, the deer's biggest threats are dogs and cars. As a result, the number of deer has increased to the point that the trees and vegetation that they feed on don't have enough opportunity to recover and are denuded.

One plant species that continues to thrive despite the munching deer population is the common blue violet. As its name suggests, the tiny plant is one of the most common wildflowers to pop up in the spring and is found in the moist woods and meadows that skirt productive marshes such as those in Ipswich.

These determined and rugged little shoots have heart-shaped leaves and five-petaled flowers, which are usually purplish blue, but can sometimes be white. Like other flower species, their petals beckon insects to venture into their reproductive system, which, if all goes well, will lead to pollination and the production of more violets. This arrangement usually works well. But if pollination isn't effective during the growing season, these violets have a superb back-up strategy to make sure they will survive.

Down lower on the stem from the main petals are compact, little bud-like flowers that look like they have yet to open. These are the self-fertilizing, or cleistogamous, flowers that aren't dependent on insects for pollination. The seeds inside these auxiliary flowers ripen right where they are and burst out of the flowers, spilling out onto the soil when they're ready to germinate. Although some seeds might be nibbled away by scavenging birds or hungry field mice, many others will settle down in the earth to take root and send more violet shoots into the warm spring air next May.

Of course, there are survival strategies and then there are Survival Strategies. If awards were given to species for long-term adaptability and survival, high on the list would have to be the alien-looking horseshoe crab. This denizen of the spring marshes and nearby estuaries has been skulking around the Earth for nearly three hundred million years—that's going back to the Paleozoic era when trilobites, nautiloid mollusks, coelacanths, and giant dragonfly larvae prowled the planet's murky waters.

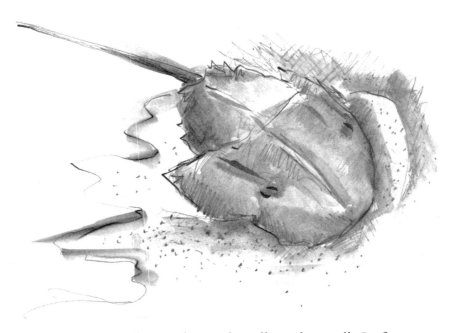

Horseshoe crabs aren't really crabs at all. In fact, their nearest living relatives are land scorpions and spiders, although unlike both they are neither venomous nor aggressive. They're of great interest to scientists and medical researchers both for their ten eyes and for their blue, copper-based blood.

Horseshoe crabs have two eyes right about where you would expect to find them on either side of their shell. These are called compound eyes. Eight of their smaller or median eyes run the length of their underside, including one on the tip of their tail. These extra eyes can detect ultraviolet light and help the crabs navigate on their annual egg-laying migrations.

Each year at this time, when the spring or highest-course tides flood the beaches from Nova Scotia to the Florida Keys, female horseshoe crabs lumber ashore with males clinging to their shells. They dig a shallow hole in the sand near the high-tide line and lay about three thousand tiny green eggs at a time. They repeat this egg-laying procedure over the next several days, laying up to eighty thousand eggs in all. Many of the eggs

will be gobbled up by shorebirds, including endangered species such as red knots and piping plovers. But the ones that make it will continue their growth cycles from egg to larvae, growing slowly but steadily until they're ready to leave the sand flats for the deeper offshore waters. Then, when mature at about ten years old, they too will repeat their species' ancient egg-laying migration with the first full moon at the spring tide.

"Conk-a-REE!" "Conk-a-REE!"

The raucous call of the red-winged blackbird greets the dawn. Migrating bands of these fiercely territorial birds are among the first to come north each spring. The males arrive a few weeks before the females in order to claim their nesting territories. When the females arrive, they set up smaller territories inside those of the males. Once that's done, things get exciting.

Because these territories are so important to the feisty males, defending them involves swooping chases and threatening calls. During these theatrical displays, the females busy themselves with gathering reeds and grasses for nest building. Because the males are polygamous, they could have as many as three different mates and three different families during the breeding season.

During their stay in the marshes, the birds will catch millions of insects to feed their hungry chicks. And in late July and August, they gather once again in secluded marshes to molt in preparation for their fall migration back to the warmer southern regions.

Elsewhere on the edge of the marsh, other new families have made their spring appearance. The eastern cottontail rabbit, with its light brown and peppery black coat is a familiar and plentiful presence. And with good reason.

The cottontail is North America's foremost prey species. In order to ensure its survival, these rabbits have a phenomenal reproduction rate. They produce as many as three litters from early spring to September.

Rabbits are most active at night. This is when they leave their forms, or nesting areas, and start looking for food. Since they're herbivores, any fresh greens, including your well-tended garden, could be up for grabs.

They also have a note-worthy digestive system. Rabbits eat the same food twice by producing two kinds of droppings. During the day, the first droppings are soft pellets, which the rabbit will eat immediately. When the pellets are digested a second time, the process breaks down more nutrients. Later, when the rabbit does its nighttime feeding, it excretes dry, brown pellets that contain the waste parts of the plants. These are the droppings you see on your lawn in the morning.

Beginning each spring, a doe, or female cottontail, gives birth to about five kits in each litter. She does this in a ready-made hole, such as a hollowed-out tree trunk or a crevice in a rock. If none of these hideouts are available, she digs a shallow scrape, or hole, in the dry ground. When the rabbits are born, they're as

naked as pink mice. They're also blind and deaf. However, within a couple of weeks these babies are mature enough to make short trips out of the nest; within a month, they are completely independent, even though they won't reach their full size for about another three months. By four months, the doe and buck, or male, are mature enough to mate and produce yet more kits on the marsh at summer's end.

Not far away, as dusk gently settles on the marsh, the mother deer and her fawn quietly nudge their way through a thicket of stalky cattails. Surrounded by sweet-smelling juniper bushes, they will lie down under the bright stars of spring and take their rest for the night.

Chapter 6

Rocks and Sand

*T*hink summer, think beaches. And without a doubt, Massachusetts has some of the finest you'll find. From Cape Cod and the Islands all the way up the coast from Revere to Salisbury, with more than 1,500 miles of tidally affected shoreline and 192 miles of open ocean coastline, there are enough beach choices to please even the most persnickety connoisseurs of sand and surf.

Some beaches are coarse sanded with tidy, uniform waves that break neatly at the shoreline; others are mercilessly jagged and stony with gorgeously clear tidepools, while still others combine New England's rocky headlands and bone-crushing waves with surprisingly soft, powdery sands.

So how did it all happen? What makes a beach like Crane or Plum Island thick with sand dunes and nary a boulder in sight while a mere two or three towns away huge granite slabs jut into the sea or golf-ball-sized rocks and stones carpet the shore?

It all goes back to glaciers. Although tides, winds, currents, and the like have their part to play in what

kind of beach you'll find and where, the last ice age did the most to carve and contour the headlands as well as dump the sand deposits that make up the rich variety of New England's beaches from Siasconset in Nantucket to Gloucester's Wingaersheek.

Remember, when the last ice age was still in full swing, sea levels were almost three hundred feet lower than they are now. That means that today's rich New England fishing grounds—Stellwagen Bank, Georges Bank, and Jeffreys Ledge—were all exposed land formations that had been repeatedly deposited and reworked during previous glacial advances and retreats.

This activity resulted in two types of coastlines— primary and secondary, or put simply, rocky and sandy. Much of New England is made up of the primary type, while the secondary would include all of Cape Cod and the Islands as well as some North Shore beaches.

As one would expect, the primary beaches like Nahant, Marblehead, and Rockport don't change much even over a long period of wind, wave, and weather action, while secondary beaches, such as Crane or Plum Island, are constantly undergoing erosions and depositions from those same forces.

Sand dunes are also the result of currents, winds, tides, and the like. They're basically hills made of wind-blown sands that build up using beach grass as a kind of armature to hold them in place. For a while.

Sand dunes migrate or move slowly downwind over time. And they can bury everything in their wind-blown path. Ragged scrub pine branches jutting up through the fine sand dunes on Crane Beach are a good example of just how efficient they can be. What appear to be waist-high shrubs are actually remains of trees up to seventy feet tall.

Drumlins, the long, tapering mounds of earth such as Hog Island or Choate Island in Ipswich, are also examples of glacial deposition and sculpting. They're the result of glacial till drawn out in the direction of the retreating ice, leaving an elongated, egg-shaped mound in its wake.

Beaches in Marblehead and Nahant are tombolo beaches, which means that they're connected to the mainland by a sand or gravel bar. Crane Beach and farther north, Salisbury Beach and Plum Island, are all

barrier beaches. These long, narrow strips of sand that lie parallel to the shore were at one time islands. During the Wisconsin Ice Age, they were cut off from the mainland by a shallow bay, which eventually filled in with sand as the sea level rose.

And although you can't swim from Halibut Point in Rockport, it's worth a visit just to experience the enormity of all that four-billion-year-old granite that holds its own against the relentless smacks of the Atlantic surf.

Chapter 7

Early Summer

Devereaux Beach, Marblehead

Sailors love Marblehead. Its deep-water harbor is splendidly protected from the ravages of fierce storms ripping up the Atlantic coast. The reason is the tombolo or stretch of rocks and sand that connects the mainland with Marblehead Neck. Devereaux Beach sits on part of that tombolo. It's a rough and tumble stony beach with a smattering of sand and a good dose of the pungent sea grass, soft sour weed that washes up with the incoming tides. By late afternoon, the local lobster fishermen are also chugging their way back to port with the tide, their boats heavy with the yield from the traps that they've been working since early dawn.

The American, New England, or northern lobster, so-called depending on where you live, is our only lobster species here in the United States. The lobster fishery is one of the few commercial fishing ventures that don't answer to pervasive multinational conglomerates. The lobsterman on the 44-foot *Patricia Louise* probably sets his traps from one to three miles out at sea. During the fall and winter months, lobsters prowl the murky depths off the Continental Shelf, but in summer they prefer the shallower, rocky ocean bottoms such as the waters beyond Marblehead's stony shores. The day's catch was a good one. His three hundred traps yielded about five hundred lobsters. Females with eggs, or coral, had to be released to ensure sound species management, especially since the odds against a lobster's survival seem dauntingly high from the outset.

A lobster egg is one of a mass made up of anywhere between five thousand and one hundred thousand eggs, depending on the female's age and prevailing environmental conditions. Of those astoundingly high egg numbers, only one percent of them will survive long enough to reach the next part of their life cycle, the planktonic or free-swimming stage. Wind and tide will exact their toll on the nascent lobsters, and predators, such as herring, mackerel, and cod, abound. During this time, the mosquito-sized lobster larvae spend most of their time swimming up and down, up and down the water column until they're ready for their next metamorphoses or change of form into the benthic, or bottom-dwelling, creature that they're meant to become.

Because lobsters have a hard, inelastic exoskeleton, or outer body, they have to shed their shell repeatedly to allow for growth and expansion. And each time they do it, they indeed do grow: up to 50% in body weight and 15% in size. They molt, or shed, up to six times during their first season, and once they reach adulthood, they will do it once or twice a year. And that can go on for a long time—some lobsters live up to a hundred years and weigh as much as forty-five pounds.

When lobsters molt, the whole shebang is renewed: claws, legs, eye stalks, antennae, everything. And should the animal lose a claw or leg during its benthic years of skirmishes and dodging prey, that too will be regenerated totally after two or three successive molts.

Lion's mane jellyfish also can be seen offshore during the summer as the waters warm up. This is a beautifully drawn creature, reddish and large with a broad, somewhat flat bell, and many, many mouth arms and tentacles that trail long and dangerously beneath the surface. Their frilly tentacles are punctuated with nematocysts, little stinging capsules that can take a swimmer quite by surprise, as this one can attest, having encountered a streaming "mane" over twelve feet long

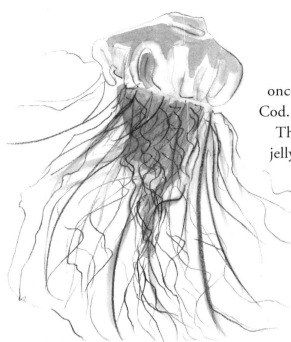

once while swimming on Cape Cod.

The Lion's mane is the largest jellyfish in the world. Although most range from about six to eighteen inches, with twelve- to twenty-foot tentacles, some have been found up to eight feet in diameter with tentacles extending sixty feet. But that's pretty rare.

As dusk settles over the leafy woodlands at the Audubon Wildlife Sanctuary on Marblehead Neck, tiny dots of bioluminescent light break through the grass and thickets at varying intervals. The seeming haphazardness of the flashes is deceptive. The blinks of light are in fact precise, timed and orchestrated even to the degree of the emitted light's intensity. Summer is here and it's mating time for fireflies.

Fireflies are not flies, but instead are in the beetle family and related to scarabs and ladybugs. What makes them beetles is the two pair of wings they tote around—one for flying and the other for protection. The firefly's light, which is produced by an organ on its abdomen, is used to find a mate; or in the case of the male firefly, a succession of mates.

Striped bass: This compact, streamlined fish, a favorite of sport and commercial fishermen, is a frequent visitor to the shallow, coastal waters north of Boston from late spring to early autumn.

Rock crab: Rock crabs are crustaceans that are often seen while snorkeling in North Shore waters. They can be found anywhere from shallow, inter-tidal pools to offshore waters in depths exceeding two thousand feet.

Green head fly: Green heads are the dreaded denizens of salt marshes and adjacent beaches. They have a brief but bitingly memorable two-week season in mid-July when the females seek out blood from unwilling donors in order to facilitate their egg production.

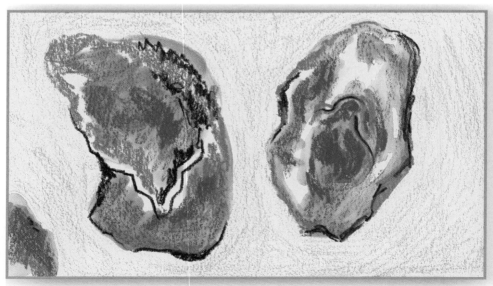

Oysters: Eastern oysters cling to shells and rocks in silty, brackish waters. Make sure you have a shellfish license if you're tempted to do any casual gathering of this tasty bivalve.

Day lilies: Originally introduced as a garden plant, day lilies escaped cultivation and now can be found blooming in stretches of open meadows as well as narrow, roadside swathes. Look for them in early summer.

Monarch butterfly: The appearance of the ephemeral monarch butterfly is one of the first sure signs of summer's end. They migrate south to Mexico often skipping one or two generations before making their return journey to New England in the spring.

Canada Geese: At one time Canada geese were considered migratory fowl in Massachusetts, with the exception of those birds daring to winter on Cape Cod. Now, great masses of them can be found throughout the year on marshes, fields, and golf courses.

Purple loostrife: Dazzling and dramatic when in bloom, this pervasive plant was originally introduced from Europe. It virtually covers most wetlands in early autumn.

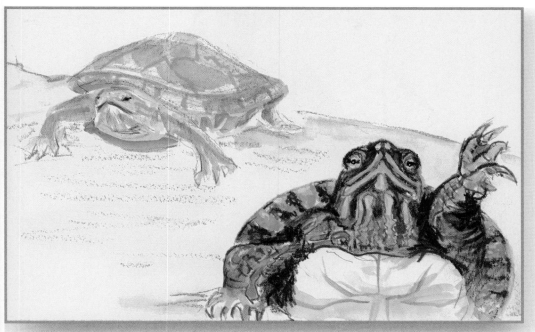

Painted turtles: Swamps, ponds, cool, wet leafy trails—these pleasant little reptiles are apt to be encountered just about anyplace other than mountains. They'll hibernate before the temperatures dip below freezing.

Cardinal: Few sights are as rewarding in the bleak of winter as that of a Northern cardinal outside one's kitchen window.

On a warm summer evening such as this, the female fireflies ready themselves on twigs and grasses, awaiting the coded signals the males send out as they fly overhead. Signals are species specific, so each firefly can readily recognize its own. When she sees a signal, a female firefly waits for an exact interval of time before responding with her own pattern of blinks. This dialogue in bioluminescent semaphore will go on several times before the male is persuaded that he's got it right and should make his cautious approach. The reason for this guarded wooing is simple. One species of firefly, the female *Photuris*, mimics the signal of other fireflies in order to attract their males, kill them, and eat them. So

the elaborate system of messaging, waiting, and re-sending of code pays off for careful males, most of the time.

Once they mate, the male will continue with his twinkling flight pattern in search of more partners. The female will not. She'll leave her perch and get ready for egg laying.

Like the lobster, fireflies also go through several metamorphoses before reaching adulthood, although their strategy is even more remarkable in its four stages.

About five days after mating, the female will lay between five hundred and a thousand eggs. Then she dies. The males have already exhausted themselves and are dead. The adult life of an insect is not a long one, generally about a month.

About thirty days after the eggs are laid, the worm-like larvae emerge and start in right away doing what they will do during this larval stage. They eat themselves silly. Since this is the time when they do most of their growing, it's important for them to find as much nourishment as possible and they do it voraciously, with snails being their particular specialty.

After molting six times while in this larval stage, changing slightly in appearance each time, the firefly prepares for its next incarnation as a pupa. It does this by burrowing into soft soil and secreting a liquid that later will harden to provide a watertight casing around the pupating insect. During this phase, the firefly will rest for about six weeks, softly glowing as it does so. When it next rouses itself, it will emerge from its co-coon as a pupa, perhaps the most dramatic phase of its metamorphosis since that's when it will begin to show characteristics of its adult form.

After remaining motionless underground for over a week, the nascent firefly starts to move once again, breaking free of its protective shell as it does so. The transformation is complete—it's now a fully equipped firefly. After resting to regain its strength, it will join its flashing companions in search of a partner on a warm summer night such as this.

Chapter 8

Late Summer

Stellwagen Bank

*I*t's a warm morning in late August and we've just left Gloucester Harbor. We're on a whale-watching cruise and headed for Stellwagen Bank. The crowd is optimistically expectant and most likely made up of more than a few who have done this before. It's hard not to become a whale junkie if you've ever had the chance to see one of these mellow leviathans mere yards from your boat.

We've gone about thirteen miles out. The combination of sounds—screeching gulls, slicing waves, and gleeful children—is a heady mix. There are scores of working birds out here, too: gulls, terns, a few greater shearwaters, and at least one Manx shearwater, all greedily swooping in on the masses of bait fish. Every keen eye on board is trained to some select spot on the stretch of open blue before the boat's prow, looking for any telltale hint of what we've all come to see. We don't have to wait long. There it is, all around us, definite signs of roiling waters. The onboard naturalist takes her cue.

"There's a big bubble ring right over here (port side) at four o'clock! And another bubble ring and a lunge at nine o'clock!" She can tell already, this is going to be a very good cruise.

Meanwhile, the boat lists under the shifting weight as dozens of eager observers shuffle about to get their bearings and a better view. And from then on it only gets better. Way better. Bubble ring blowing, breaching, fluking, spy hopping, flipper slapping—there's an entire vocabulary devoted to describing the behavioral displays these animals exhibit, and the observers on this cruise are getting to see them all. The main event is the placid and obliging humpback whale.

Humpback whales make up the clear majority of the whales that frequent these northern Atlantic waters in the summer. The day we went out, we saw forty of them, an exceptionally good count, we were told. There were also three finbacks and a minke whale thrown in for good measure.

Like all the cetacean or whale species, humpbacks are mammals, not fish. They breathe air, are warm blooded, have (some) hair, and give birth to and suckle their young. Recent fossil findings suggest that roughly fifty million years ago, whales shared a common ancestor with animals such as sheep, goats, camels, and deer. Furthermore, it's surmised that as they branched off and adapted to aquatic life they very gradually evolved the features we see today—fins, flukes, tails, no legs.

Adult humpback whales are not the largest—that distinction belongs to the blue whale—but they're still pretty darn big. An adult humpback is about fifty feet long and weighs twenty-five to forty tons. It has four fins: two ventral or side flippers, which are the longest of any whale species, up to eighteen feet; one dorsal fin; and its tail or flukes.

Humpbacks are baleen, or toothless, whales. They have four hundred plates of baleen hanging from their upper jaws that is composed of keratin, the same material as your fingernails and hair. Humpbacks are also in the Rorqual family, a subset of the baleens that have deep folds or pleats under their chins that go all the way down to their navels. These folds expand, like a pelican's lower pouch. When they do that, they can let in huge amounts of water, up to fifteen thousand gallons. This water is thick with fish and plankton. The whale then squeezes the water out through its baleen plates, straining out the food.

Humpbacks have two blowholes on the top of their head; some species of cetacean, including dolphins, just have one. Whales have to hold their breath when diving for their food, which can take them from four to ten minutes to gather; they're able to do that because the air goes directly to their lungs. Before they dive, the blowhole is completely sealed off. That's how they can open their mouths for food.

When they surface, they expel all that air, which has been warming inside their capacious lungs and so is released as huge plumes of steam, rising as high as twenty feet and visible for up to a mile.

When a whale is engaged in bubble ring activity, it's actually fashioning an enormous air cage made out of bubbles in order to trap massive schools of herring and acres of plankton blooms. Several whales work together to accomplish this, with one swimming and blowing bubbles under a school of fish to form the ring while the others make noise to startle the fish to the surface. When they get there, the whales are ready with mouths wide open to welcome them in.

A whale's blubber, or subcutaneous tissue, is rich in fat and oil. It's the reason the whale stays warm and also how it stays alive over the long winter months when it goes south to mate and give birth to its young.

Whales don't eat much as they travel to their winter homing grounds in the Caribbean and virtually not at all during their stay there. This makes these summer trips to the rich feeding grounds off the Cape Ann shores all the more crucial over the long term for their survival.

There's much about whales that's completely unknown or left to conjecture. Maybe that's part of the curious appeal they wield. How do they navigate such vast distances? Why are they so vocal? Why do they sometimes beach themselves despite repeated efforts to lead them back to open seas?

Some theories suggest that whales follow impulses emitted from the Earth's magnetic field as a means of navigating as well as following primary ocean currents. A whale's hearing is rather spectacular, too. It has been said that its entire body actually feels sound, which explains why it gathers its most essential information in that manner. And as for singing, humpbacks are the divas of the sea.

No one is quite sure why they sing, but since it's the males that do so, speculation runs high that it has something to do with courtship behavior. Their songs are long, up to twenty minutes, and complex in

arrangement. They're also specific to coast—Atlantic humpbacks sing a different tune than their cousins in the Pacific Ocean, and the songs also vary in composition from year to year on both coasts.

An unexpected bonus on this cruise was the sighting of a pod, or group, of about thirty white-sided Atlantic dolphins. Also in the cetacean family, these sleek mammals glide through the surf with a graceful abandon that's a joy to watch. They're between 5 and 8 feet long, weigh up to 600 pounds, and show a distinctive white and yellow stripe on either side. They feed on the herring that the whales gobble up but they'll also go for squid and other small fish like smelt, silver hake, and shrimp. Preferring the colder waters, these nimble dolphins range from southern New England all the way up to Norway.

As the boat turns around to head back to port, humpbacks can still be seen spy hopping, or rising vertically out of the water to take a look around while others continue with their bubble net activities. All the while, seabirds are everywhere, trying to cash in on all that good splashing and water slapping that's bringing so much food up to the surface.

As on land, so here on water, gulls are ubiquitous. One of the most pervasive of the species, herring gulls, are all around, screeching and squabbling for every morsel and tidbit that doesn't find its way down a whale's gullet. One can't help but admire their feistiness. Gulls are scavengers—no big surprise there— and will eat everything from insects to carrion and a bit of garbage thrown in on the side. Their feathers are waterproof, and if you've ever wondered how they always manage to look so clean and spiffy despite their nasty eating venues, it's due to a combination of oil glands and preening. The gulls secrete an oil from the base of their tails, which they use to daub all over their feathers. They also molt twice a year, in spring and fall, which helps to give them that dapper appearance.

Gulls are attentive and protective parents. Both male and female will feed and guard their brood, usually made up of three chicks, rarely leaving them alone. They fend off potential marauders such as fox, owls, or dogs, by fiercely beating their sizeable wings; however, they're not above preying on the chicks of other gulls if they get the chance.

Gulls are one of the most resourceful birds on the planet and if they had hands we'd be in trouble. Don't leave your food unattended on the beach. Unless it's zipped, locked, and hidden, they'll find it and eat it. Actually, don't even bother. They'll get to it anyway.

Chapter 9

Great Marsh

Five snowy egrets soar in an exquisite constellation above the deepening blue waters that edge the Essex marsh. By summer's end, the colors that course through the marshlands have gone from the sweet-pea greens of early June to the ripe, verdant emeralds of August, and on to the russet-gold sienna of early October. Easily rivaling the brash drama of the region's rocky headlands, the quiet splendor of the Great Marsh winds its way through seven privileged towns and five rivers.

The Great Marsh is made up of twenty-five thousand acres of some of the most significant ecosystems in the northeast sector of the continent. Essex, Ipswich, Gloucester, Rowley, Newbury, and Newburyport all have notable claims to the marsh, which extends northward into southern New Hampshire, and all of the towns profit from its proximity as an ecotourism destination and as a valuable shellfishery source.

The importance of marshes anywhere on Earth can't be underrated. The reason has to do with how they're formed and various functions they serve.

Just as in beach formation, the Great Marsh has its genesis in the retreat of the Laurentide ice sheet that covered much of the continent. The melting glacier resulted in the terminal moraines of Long Island, Cape Cod, Martha's Vineyard, and Nantucket, as well as the numerous river systems, bays, inlets, estuaries, and barrier islands all along the eastern seaboard.

Over time, incoming and outgoing ocean tides slowly brought a combination of sand and mud sediments from inland riverways to fill in these bays and estuaries until they were finally at level with the sea at high tide. But they didn't start looking like the marshes we recognize until the appearance of marsh grasses. The first to show up on the scene was eelgrass. Since it can live in an entirely underwater habitat, it was the perfect ingredient for getting the marshes up and running. After that, many marine organisms took up residence, enriching the anaerobic mud with their remains as they spun out their life cycles.

Spartina alterniflora grass—which may have been carried in as a seed stuck to the foot of some visiting bird—germinated, grew, flourished, and still is a main-

stay for many marsh creatures. These specialized plants have shallow roots and hollow stems. *Spartina patens*, or marsh hay, grows farther inland on the marsh, as does *Salicornia*, or glasswort, a tasty succulent.

By its very nature as a wetland, the marsh is covered with either salt- or fresh water most of the time. Trees can't grow in a marsh but in addition to the spartina grasses, there are lots of reeds, brushes, cattails, and some flowering plants.

Marshes and freshwater wetlands act like gigantic sponges. During torrential rains, they protect nearby locales from flooding and they also lessen the full brunt of ocean storms, acting as buffer zones.

But that's nothing compared to their value as habitats to scores of bird, fish, insect, amphibian, reptile, and other wildlife species. The significance of the Great Marsh was readily apparent to the Native American peoples who lived, hunted, fished, and farmed in the region prior to its colonization by European settlers. The revered Agawam chief, Masconomo,

was overseer to all the lands included in the marsh. A memorial to him can be found on Sagamore Hill in Hamilton.

Colonists depended on the Great Marsh for their salt hay, which they used for everything from insulation to bedding. It also provided a nutrient-rich feed for their livestock, which in turn produced vitamin-rich milk.

There was a time, not very long ago, when wetlands were deemed to be wastelands suitable only for building development or landfill dumps. Such myopic planning can be catastrophic, as we witnessed in the Louisiana delta, post–Hurricane Katrina in 2005.

Happily, much of the Great Marsh is under federal protection as an Area of Critical Environmental Concern (ACEC) to ensure its ongoing role as one of the richest natural habitats in the world.

Chapter 10

Early Autumn

Route 1A–Rowley, Newbury, Newburyport

W e have friends who have done their safari bit in equatorial Africa. They've dived on the Great Barrier Reef in Australia. Heck, they even own a catamaran that they keep in the Kingdom of Tonga. They do their share of exotic jaunts and when they do, it's not the wussy, pre-packaged, fake-it-as-you-go kind. They go native and do Rough Ride not Blue Book. In short, it's all the travel that's still on my "to do" list.

But as I'm driving down Route 1A, heading north out of Rowley in our bare-boned, second-hand jeep, I can't help but smile in a goofy sort of awe at what I see around me. And what I see is completely surrounding this twisting back road like a tapestried shawl. Right here are unrivaled adventures for the taking. Right here in this astounding beauty of tawny marshlands that spread out before me like a lavish Sunday picnic.

No lions crouch in the veldt or manta rays skulk in the reefs, true. But the bounty of life forms thriving all around these luxuriant, grassy waters is plenty grand, nonetheless.

Consider Quascacunquen. Native Americans referred to this part of the Great Marsh by that tongue twister because it means "waterfall" and, fittingly, it straddles the falls of the Parker River. This sweep of marshlands and tidal creeks is now known by the prosaic moniker of Old Town Hill. Because of its unusual configuration—it's a glacial drumlin that's part marine, part moor or upland—it supports an equally unusual mix of habitats. Frequent wildlife visitors include raptors such as northern harriers, red-tailed hawks, ospreys, owls, great and snowy egrets, and everyone's favorite outsize avian, the great blue heron.

These birds are always labeled in superlatives. Largest herons in North America. Most well known. Most pervasive heron in North America. But in fact, great blue herons, or Big Crankys as they're called in some backwaters, are very cool birds to observe in the marsh.

Standing between three and four feet tall and flexing a wingspan that reaches outward of five feet ten inches, these birds are more reminiscent of Jurassic Park than Central Park. Their distinctive appearance—blue-grey feathers, set off by a long, thick, yellow bill and attenuated twiggy legs—is made all the more primordial when you see them take off. And when flying, as when at rest, the great blue heron holds it coiled length of neck in a rather jaunty "S" curve.

Great blues are at home in both salt and freshwater marshes and swamps. The best time to see them is when they're cruising, or stalking, for their meals; that's usually in the morning and at dusk when fishing is optimal. Their hunting strategies are twofold. Either they'll stand absolutely still in the shallows until some hapless fish swims close by, or they'll nonchalantly saunter through the waters until they spot something that looks appealing to them. In addition to fish, they eat insects, reptiles, mice, and when near freshwater, their favorite entree, frogs.

Great blue herons are not favored in great numbers, as close to 70% of the hatchlings die in their first year. The oldest-known bird reached the ripe old age of twenty-three, but fifteen seems to be about their average life span.

Thanks to sanctuaries like the Parker River National Wildlife Refuge, many species such as the great blue heron have a better chance of not just surviving but flourishing. More than four thousand acres of unspoiled habitat offers crucial resting, nesting, and feeding grounds to a vast array of wildlife. Three hundred species of birds as well as large numbers of plants, mammals, reptiles, amphibians, and insects take advantage of its wetlands, bogs, fresh- and saltwater marshes, creeks, rivers, and mud flats during migration and as permanent residents.

Here, the green darner dragonfly will ready itself to begin its long migration south. Dragonflies are ancient creatures. They are also some of the most stunningly dazzling insects in the phylum. The green darner is no exception. It's one of the largest and easiest to identify of the thirty-eight dragonfly species that frequent the United States. Its four-inch-long iridescent wings are a phenomenal marriage of elegance in design and engineering. Its body is almost as long as its wingspread and its eyes are spherical and compound.

Dragonflies are the sexual acrobats of the insect world. They mate just as readily in mid-air as on the ground or suspended from a leafy branch.

After mating, a female finds a plant growing in the water. While holding onto a stalk of the grass, she slowly inches her way backwards into the water while at the same time incising the plant's stem so that she can lay her eggs in it.

When the larvae, known as naiads, later hatch, they prove to be mean little cusses that will attack just about anything that comes across their transom. They go for tadpoles, insects, and even earthworms, should they happen to find themselves washed into the watery mix.

Naiads molt their protective shells many times before they finally tread their way to daylight on the stem of a plant. When they do, they emerge in adult form with unspeakably beautiful diaphanous wings and the appetite of a truck driver. If you don't like mosquitoes and midges, this dragonfly is your best friend. Of course, they also eat wasps, butterflies, bees, and perhaps some other dragonflies. When they migrate south, they do so en masse, and they won't come back. But their progeny will, to repeat the whole process all over again.

Less obvious but just as remarkable a resident is the humble mud dog whelk. Known more commonly as mud snails, these little scavengers patiently pursue their found meals using chemoreceptors, cells that respond to chemical stimulus, which are located on the outside of their bodies. They wave their pointy little proboscis, a tube at the front end of the snail with its mouth right behind it, in front of them as they trawl the soft, muddy shallows of the bays and inlets, and the chemoreceptor picks up what kind of chemicals are in the water.

The interesting thing is that, unlike many scavengers who are not known for their discriminating food choices, mud snails won't eat their own dead. Research suggests that the chemical scent of their own kind not doing so well might act as a red flag, telling them to watch out for possible predators in their vicinity so that they won't meet a similar doom.

A dizzying range of birds flocks to the Plum Island Great Marsh—everything from waterfowl, to passerines, to shorebirds, to raptors, and all deserve their own chapter. But picking a raptor at random, the northern harrier is a solid choice. For one thing, it's the only North American member of a group of hawks that have the dubious distinction of being called "harriers." The term comes by way of an old English word that means to harass or ravage, which is funny when you think about it because, well, don't all raptors do that to their prey? Anyway, these northern harriers do it differ-

ently than their less-harassing (one supposes) hawkish cousins.

For one thing, harriers use their excellent sense of hearing, something other hawks can't brag about. That's because their faces are rather disc-shaped, like an owl's, which helps to intensify the sound coming at them with directional range.

Rather than stalking their prey—mice, insects, frogs, baby birds—from a great distance or from an observation perch the way most raptors do, harriers fly very close to the ground and swoop in, kamikaze-style, to snag their catch by surprise.

Harriers breed in colonies, usually familiar territories, roosting and nesting on the ground. They're notably nimble, for hawks, and perform an intricate aerial courtship display made up of lots of loopy twists and turns.

The combined impact of habitat loss, use of dangerous pesticides, and the wanton development of wetland areas have all taken their toll on the population numbers of harrier hawks. Thankfully, none of those reach the Parker River Wildlife Refuge.

Chapter 11

Late Autumn

Eastern Point, Gloucester

*I*t's late afternoon on the last day of October. Maybe it's the slate cast to a gloomy sky, or maybe it just comes from living in Gloucester, but locals at the Dunkin' Donuts are invoking memories of the "Perfect Storm." That was the fatal nor'easter that swallowed up six Gloucester fishermen and their vessel, the *Andrea Gail*, in the furious waters off Cape Sable on Halloween night, 1991.

Maybe that's also why these spectral memories of a town and its uneasy alliance with the wide open Atlantic lead to ready comparisons on the ride to the Eastern Point Lighthouse and Dog Bar Breakwater. Sure enough, they pop up like dialogue boxes starting at the entrance to Eastern Point Boulevard.

Eastern Point is a closed, private enclave. Two stone pillars command the point's access like mute sentries. "Private Property—No Trespassing" notices are as frequent on lawns as picket signs in an election year. The boulevard is studded with imposing estates, left and

right, old and new, that dwarf the surrounding land and seascape. At one time, the entire point had been a single working farm, the largest in Gloucester. Then, as seaside resorts were taking hold in the public imagination in the late nineteenth century, some developer with an eye for waterfront property and its future exponential value increase must have had an "a-ha!" moment and the rest is, well, "no trespassing" signs and stone pillars.

But the lighthouse, rebuilt in 1890, and Dog Bar Breakwater, a half-mile causeway comprised of Rockport granite laid down on top of a hazardous sandbar, are under the jurisdiction of the U.S. Coast Guard. The fifty-three-acre wildlife preserve that surrounds this stunning slice of granite and sea is owned by the

Massachusetts Audubon Society. Which is good news, since in addition to being one of the most dramatic viewpoints to Gloucester Harbor and the expanse of open ocean, this is also one humdinger of a place to see migrating waterfowl, shorebirds, seabirds, and monarch butterflies.

At low tide, the salty air is thick with the lush perfume of at least four different kinds of seaweeds. Codium, Irish moss, rockweed, and dulse are festooned decoratively across the rocky beach, protected by the breakwater. Scooping up double fistfuls of these tangled algae and breathing in their scent is fall's equivalent of gathering wildflowers in late spring. From the variegated greens and browns to the soft reds and purples, this

ephemeral bouquet is very Cape Ann.

Eider ducks, sea ducks, black ducks, and white-winged scoters are all visitors to these waters during this time of year. Some will stay over the winter if it's not too harsh, while others will wend their way south to the Chesapeake Bay.

Shorebirds are also big fans of the Sanctuary waters. Purple sandpipers, dunlins, Bonaparte gulls, kittiwakes, loons, razorbills, and the quick-change artist (well, sort of quick), the black guillemot are frequent residents.

The black guillemot is in the puffin family, though measuring at about one foot in length, they're slightly larger than their puffin cousins. Their distinctive plumage—overall black except for white patches in each wing and underwing coverts—goes through a radical change during the winter: The black turns to white with bits of black sprinkled about here and there, giving them a somewhat mottled appearance.

Theirs is a pelagic species, which means the black guillemot will spend most of its life out at sea, except when it's time to mate. Then it will look for rocky shores strewn with craggy boulders and cliffs to make its nest.

These monogamous birds breed in small colonies of about a dozen and are fiercely territorial and devoted to their nesting sites, often returning to the same place year after year. Both sexes share in incubating the clutch, usually of two eggs, and also in catching up to twenty fish a day for the ravenous chicks once they've hatched.

Guillemots are deep surface divers, up to a hundred feet, and can stay submerged for up to two minutes. They eat a varied menu, mostly small fish such as sand lance and sculpins, but they're not above foraging for crabs, jellyfish, and sponges. Guillemots often stay the winter in their nesting areas, moving out to open waters if food is in short supply, but they seldom migrate very far south.

The northern gannet is another pelagic bird that can often be spotted swooping through these waters in late autumn. This aerodynamically charged, gull-like bird is designed like the paper airplane you always wished you could fold. Looking at it from below, it resembles a four-pointed star or a delta fighter, and considering its food gathering technique, that makes perfect sense. Gannets feed on mackerel and herring, fish that usually school near the surface. The gannet, with its

wingspan
of close to five feet,
will drop down vertically from a
lofty one to two hundred feet in the air,
plummeting into the thick of a school of star-
tled fishes like a sniper's bullet. As one might expect,
the gannet's sleek skull is also well designed to absorb
the impact of these hair-splitting dives by means of a
system of air sacs. Gannets spend their winters at sea as
far south as the Gulf of Mexico.

Around the jutting curve of stony shoreline from the
lighthouse, the waning November sun casts its sharp
mustard-colored light onto Rocky Neck's scanty beach.
It's low tide and a young harbor seal has hauled its
weight onto an exposed boulder near the shallows
to catch a few more warming rays before a fast-
approaching dusk falls.

Harbor seals are numerous and
frequent winter residents in the com-
paratively warm waters of Cape Ann and
farther south to Cape Cod. They summer in

the cooler north from northern Maine to southern Canada. That's also when they mate and bear their young in the scattered islands off the coasts of southern New Hampshire and Maine as well as here in Massachusetts. The female gives birth to a single pup that is fully furred and an eager and adept swimmer right from birth.

Harbor seals are in the Phocidae or true seal family because, unlike sea lions and fur seals, they don't have external ears that stick out. Another feature that sets them apart from these notorious performers on the entertainment circuit is their inability to hoist themselves up on their back flippers—they just aren't built that way.

These playful mammals range in color from light gray to brown to charcoal and everything in between. Their plaintive black eyes, set in a wide, neckless face,

bear an uncanny resemblance to the family dog—to our family dog, at any rate. Harbor seals feed on fish, mollusks, and crustaceans, and dive as deep as three hundred feet to find their meals and stay submerged for up to half an hour. This visiting seal to Rocky Neck will slip off into the blackening night as the returning tide comes in once again, making its way back noiselessly to the rich fishing grounds of Stellwagen Bank.

Chapter 12

Stellwagen Bank

42°25' Latitude, 70°25' Longitude

Not to belittle Henry Stellwagen, but I'll wager that if Native Americans had been the first to officially map the 842 square miles skirting the fringes of Massachusetts Bay, they would have come up with something more evocative than the eponymous "Stellwagen Bank." Maybe a name that meant something like "underwater mesa teeming with myriad life forms." Something that would remind the human coastal inhabitants of the wealth of treasures swarming through their offshore waters.

The Stellwagen Bank National Marine Sanctuary, though not a title tripping off the tongue, does that in some measure by its federally protected status.

This offshore sanctuary includes all of Stellwagen and Tilles Bank as well as parts of Jeffreys Ledge, from three miles southeast of Cape Ann to three miles north of Cape Cod and twenty-five miles off of Boston.

This subaquatic plateau made up of sand and gravel is home, nursery, feeding ground, and migration

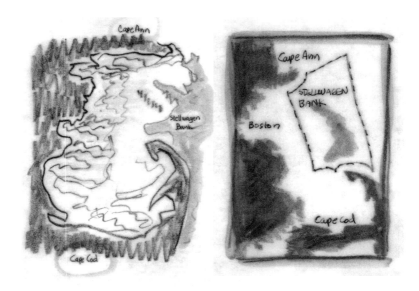

route for, well, you name it: humpback, finback, and North Atlantic right whales; silver hake, Atlantic cod, yellowtail flounder, squid, lobsters, sea scallops, striped bass, bluefin tuna; a whole bunch of seabirds such as gannets, shearwaters, puffins, jaegers, razorbills, as well as terns, marine ducks, and geese; leatherbacks and Kemp's Ridley sea turtles; harbor seals and Atlantic white-sided dolphins. And that by no means exhausts the bulky list.

The abundance of wildlife has to do with the variety of benthic (bottom-dwelling) and pelagic (open-ocean) habitats that this astounding area encompasses. And that goes back, yet again, to glaciation.

Remember, back when the Laurentide ice sheet extended its frozen reach from Canada down through

New England about twenty thousand years ago, the global sea level was about three hundred feet lower than it is today.

As the ice melted over a period of some eight thousand years, Stellwagen Bank was way above sea level and may even have been connected to lower Cape Cod. Indeed, if you look at a topographical map of the area, the bank looks like a copy of the Cape's flexed outer arm. Twelve thousand years ago, the bank probably shared many surface features with that sandy spit of terminal moraine: marshes, swamps, lakes, and beaches as well as tundra vegetation were probably all recognizable features of the bank.

Remember, too, that this is where both mastodon and mammoth teeth were unearthed some twelve thousand years later.

But back to glacial melt-down. As the sea level continued to rise, the land mass that made up the bank slowly but steadily was enveloped by the melting waters until ten thousand years ago, when it was completely submerged. Then the waves and currents took over and removed a little here, added a bit there, and slowly carved and fashioned the bank as it is today. Ridges, troughs, canyons, rocky ledges, gorges, muddy basins, and even glacial boulder fields make up this wildly diverse habitat. And that's why so many different plants and animals thrive here.

Water depths at the surface of the bank range from

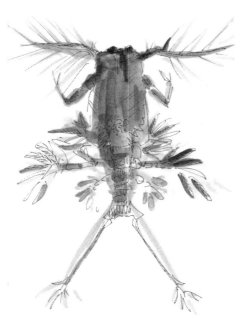

65 to 100 feet, while depths in the basins of the bank can plunge to about 260 feet. An oceanographic feature known as upwelling stirs and mixes nutrient-rich waters from the warm surface with the colder water from the ocean floor to serve up a smorgasbord with wide appeal to its residents and visitors.

Tiny algae-like plants called phytoplankton use the Sun's energy to grow, while zooplankton, which can include anything from tiny copepods to animals such as gastropods in their larval stage, in turn feed on the phytoplankton blooms. From there, the food chain goes up and up to leviathans that feast on waters thick with sand lance. It's an elegantly efficient system.

Henry Stellwagen mapped the bank in 1854. He was a U.S. Navy lieutenant on loan to the Coast Survey to scout out potential lighthouse locales. While doing so, he figured out the idiosyncratic feature of the bank that hadn't been put on any official maps. This was a pretty big deal in the radar- and sonar-less 1800s, since mariners only had a weighted line lowered into the water to tell them what sort of depths they were getting into. With the mapping of Stellwagen Bank, ship captains now would know when they were leaving the deeper waters of the Gulf of Maine for the tricky and treacherous waters of Boston Harbor, not an easy place to navigate in the best of situations, let alone in the dark and fog. At least fifty shipwrecks on the bank bear silent witness to that detail.

Today, Stellwagen Bank is as bustling on the surface as it is below, serving as major shipping lanes to Boston, a viable commercial and sport fishing ground, and an enormously popular whale-watching venue with international name recognition. Well done, Henry.

Chapter 13

Early Winter

Beverly Conservation Area

*I*t's early winter and a few dingy brown leaves are still clinging to the grey branches like ragged laundry on a line. Successive nighttime frosts have tightened the soil so that instead of a spring, footfalls tend to tamp and make a noise they didn't just the month before. The sound of a snapping twig has more crackle, a crow's cawing carries more menace, and a coyte's howl tugs at the imagination in a disconcerting way. It's just plain spooky. Especially here in the woods at two o'clock in the morning.

The first yelp seems to erupt in the black air out of one place and no place. Then, barely on the heels of its second cry, two, three, maybe even a half-dozen howls, wails, and eerie moans coming from coyotes hidden in the shadows tear at the quiet of the night with fierce determination. This goes on for maybe forty-five seconds. Then they stop. And start. And stop again. Then they exit the way they entered, with stealth and admittedly, more than a little style.

Native American myths about the First People abound with allusions to "the trickster," often represented by the coyote because of his wily, cunning, and scavenging ways. The name "coyote" comes by way of the Mexican Aztec word for the animal they called *coyotl,* and like jackals, wolves, and fox, they all share a common ancestry with dogs.

These amazingly adaptive animals from the western prairies made their way east, perhaps breeding with timber wolves in the Great Lakes region and showing up in New York State in the 1920s.

Eastern coyotes are larger than their western counterparts, standing about two feet tall and upwards of four feet long, including their big, bushy tail. At first glance, you could mistake one for a German shepherd—long, thick, yellow-grey fur, upright ears—but the coyote has a much more pronounced point to its

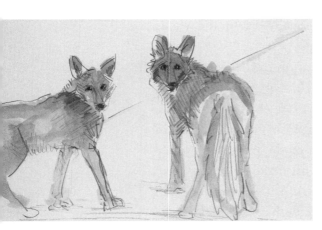

muzzle and its gait is more of a wolfy lope. Unlike a wolf, however, it doesn't hold its tail straight out, or like a dog, curled up behind, but rather keeps it straight down near its hindquarters.

Coyotes are masters of adaptability and survival as their wide range of

habitat attest. They can be found in rural forests as well as populous suburbs. And they'll eat anything: shrews, birds, voles, beaver, deer, insects, lizards, and frogs. If their prey is already dead, so much the better. If they have to hunt for it, and they generally hunt alone, it's most likely going to be small, easy game like mice and shrews. Sometimes a pack will orchestrate a hunt to bring down a big animal such as a stressed deer, but that's the rare exception, not the rule.

An index to their intelligence is the amount of parental investment both sexes commit. Coyotes are mostly monogamous and will stay with the same partner for several mating seasons, sometimes for life. They mate sometime in February in the cold northeast, and start working on their den come March. A litter of four to a dozen, but usually around seven pups, is born in April. Both parents are very attentive. The father has his own den nearby but is nevertheless on constant patrol to guard the family den and bring back food to the pups once they've been weaned. He also teaches the young'uns how to

hunt, starting off with tasty insects to hone their skills. And although their eyesight isn't especially sharp, their sense of smell and hearing is acute. This makes them adept hunters suited to whatever environment they choose to take residence in.

And the howling? It's a way to keep in touch in the dark. Or just to say hi. Coyotes like to know who's where, especially if they're on a group hunt. They also bark, growl, and yelp under various circumstances. And sometimes, they simply throw back their heads to howl for the sheer joy of it.

About fifteen miles northwest in a Boxford thicket of hemlocks and spruce trees, a great horned owl can be heard but not seen. Its melancholy whoo-who-who-who-whooo's carry all the way through the moonless night down the gravel driveway leading to a boggy swamp. The great horned is the largest of the American "eared" owls, standing at over two feet tall with a four-and-a-half-foot wingspan. This nocturnal raptor is an efficient hunter and eats almost as varied a diet as the coyote, with rabbits, frogs, beetles, and lizards included on its menu. The great horned owl is one of the first birds to nest and will lay its eggs as early as January despite a snow-covered landscape.

In nearby Topsfield, the daylight hours have done their best to warm crusty pond edges and scarlet winterberry bushes with wan rays of distant sunshine. It's not yet four P.M., but the winter solstice has yet to mark the turnaround with hopes of spring.

At a small juncture on the road that borders the Ipswich River, a dark brown shape about the size of a housecat slithers quickly across the road to the safety of the icy water. This is the fisher cat, not a cat at all, but a member of the weasel family and looking every bit the part. The Chippewa called them *tha-cho*, which means "big marten," their weasely cousins. Actually, fishers are about twice the size of martens, but they share the recognizable characteristics of a long, pliant body, short legs, long tail, and small, round ears.

Fishers share reproductive strategies with martens, other weasels, and river otters. They mate in early spring and after the fertilized eggs develop for a few weeks they just stop developing. Nine months later, in winter, the eggs resume their development and a few months after that, some 350 days after mating, the mother gives birth to a litter of three wee fishers. Biologists speculate that this interrupted development scheme must in some way boost their odds of survival.

Unlike the dutiful coyote male, the fisher dad doesn't hang around at all. In fact, the mother doesn't do much homemaking either. Right after she gives birth, she leaves the den to mate again. The young fishers will stay in the den with her (when she's around), and she'll show them the ropes of hunting until the following fall. Then they're on their own.

The fisher population took a big hit in the 1920s when the animals were practically wiped out for their luxurious fur pelts. Females were especially sought after for their lustrously dark coats.

Trapping the animals was outlawed by the 1930s and their numbers rebounded. Fishers play an important role in maintaining a healthy balance in many woodland areas where porcupines have reached nuisance proportions.

Few animals are gutsy and quick enough to take on porcupines, but the fisher does it with alacrity. Porcupines may be cute, but they can do considerable damage by chewing on wooden road signs, trees, and rubber tires and wiring, as well as the inner bark of trees. Maybe because they're known to scrap so adroitly with porcupines, fishers have earned an unmerited reputation for wanton nastiness, but in fact most of the time they're doing well if they get a red squirrel or two for their meal.

As the late afternoon sun is quenched by the horizon at a woodland's edge in North Andover, a red-tailed hawk lazily follows its trajectory. Its burnished auburn tail feathers catch the retreating light, advertising its descriptive name. This hefty raptor, one of the largest seen year-round in New England, is in the buzzard and eagle family. Like the eagle, it's outfitted with a fiercely hooked beak and razor-sharp talons at the end of powerfully built legs and feet. These claws are its undisputed weapons and hunting tools.

The red-tailed hawk is almost always seen in the company of crows, grackles, and ravens. And not because they're all buddies. Far from it. Their aerial skirmishes go way back. Crows have a particular loathing for these hawks and will squawk at them with vicious abandon as they mob or chase them away from their turf. Crows also steal the hawk's eggs and kill their chicks if they can get to its nest. Needless to say, if the hawk gets hold of the crow, it rips it apart.

This hawk will continue its mid-winter search for any small rodents in its keen field of vision until it reaches its nest and waiting mate.

Folly Hill, Danvers

The top of Folly Hill is an outstanding place to pull up a chair, grab a blanket, and tilt your head back. This hill—drumlin, actually—commands one of the most spectacular views of Essex County, spanning nearly a fifty-mile circumference: to the east the shining Atlantic, to the west the forests, meadows, and marshes of the surrounding towns.

Nathaniel Hawthorne had fond memories of the place that he put in a charming little missive to his cousin, referring to it by its older designation, Browne's Folly. It was Browne's Folly because one William Browne of Salem town built a sprawling and grandiose (by Puritan New England standards) trophy house on the brow of the hill for his fourteen-year-old bride.

The estate was virtually destroyed, as were many other homes, in the great Cape Ann earthquake of 1755. Local clergy and lay people alike were convinced it was the work of a punitive God venting anger at just such venial ostentation as Messer Brown displayed in his flamboyant architecture. Cooler heads tried to engage reason. Harvard professor of Mathematics and

Philosophy, John Winthrop, tactfully offered that maybe the quake was some sort of fierce chemical and heat thing going on deep underground.

Actually, the epicenter of the quake was about twenty-five miles out to sea, east-northeast of Cape Ann. Passengers aboard a vessel near the hot spot were sure they had run aground during the tremors and were very much surprised and probably pretty happy to find themselves safely entering Boston Harbor waters later that day. Indeed, the Cape Ann quake was felt as far north as Montreal and south to the Chesapeake. No small shiver this.

When as teenagers we ventured up to the hilltop, it was referred to as "the cake pan," so named for the mundane-looking water tower that wryly commanded the landscape. Now the hill is a mosaic of housing units called Folly Hill Apartments. Still, the sky's the thing this winter night.

The Geminid meteor showers are like early Christmas presents. Better, since they're free and available to everyone. They transit the deep, mid-December skies and are exquisitely wrapped in grand anticipation and unearthly splendor.

Unlike their more celebrated counterparts—the Perseids and the Leonids—the Geminid meteor showers weren't even on our radar screens until 1862, when ten to twenty shooting stars—meteors to be more precise—were observed flashing across the heavens within the space of an hour. Their radiant, or point of origin, is in the constellation Gemini, hence the name. But there's still controversy about the source of the Geminid shower.

In 1983, the National Aeronautics and Space Administration (NASA) determined that the Geminid shower was coming from 3200 Phaethon. But was Phaethon a comet or a rocky asteroid? Meteor showers are basically the rubbly junk cast off of comets that venture too close to the Sun. Comets are mostly made up of ice and dust—"dirty snowballs" is the catch

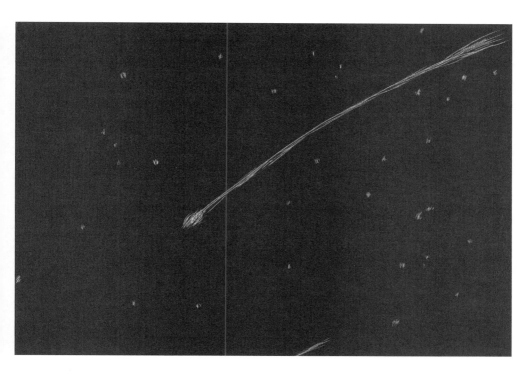

phrase. But if the shower is coming from an asteroid, no one is quite sure just how it works. Asteroids are small, weirdly shaped rocks that loiter in the inner solar system, mainly in an asteroid neighborhood known as the Kuiper belt.

Some scientists say there really isn't a clear distinction between the two entities. Many other astronomers have simplified the argument, concluding that some asteroids, perhaps including 3200 Phaethon, are actually dead or inactive comets that simply amassed a lot of interplanetary dust in their cosmic travels. In other words, what looks like an asteroid acts like a comet.

Hairsplitting over nomenclature aside, the Geminid shower has been intensifying steadily, making it one of the most spectacular meteor showers earthlings get to witness. And on a moonless, cloud-free December night, the display of these streaming shards of light can awaken childlike wonder in even the most curmudgeonly of stiffs.

Chapter 14

Late Winter

Bald Hill East, Boxford

By the second week in January, daylight has lengthened by several minutes. But winter is winter. For the casual observer, not much has changed since the solstice. Maybe its colder and there's probably more snow to shovel.

On a bright icy day, the snow-covered trees and the path leading to the pond are splashed with the sky's endless arc of blue. Sounds leap out of the air unbidden: the squeak of snow underfoot, the tisking of a chickadee, and a grackle's squawk of disdain. The air is scented with that perfect cold purity of juniper and pine that makes all the vexing details of New England winters seem forgivable. The path leading to the embankment is rife with beaver work. Trees have been gnawed, limbs stripped and chewed, and a stew of twigs and wood chips litters the slushy ground.

The semi-aquatic beaver is the largest rodent in North America, standing at sixteen inches tall and

about three and a half feet long. Its hind feet are webbed, its front teeth grow constantly, and its paddle-shaped tail is legendary. It also has specially adapted features for its intense underwater lifestyle, such as clear eyelids, nostrils equipped with valves that shut, lips that close behind its orange teeth, and an abundant coat of thick, oily fur that provides excellent insulation. If it had to, the beaver could stay submerged for up to fifteen minutes.

Busy and beaver, beaver and busy—the two words really do seem meant for each other. But the beavers' compulsive tree stripping and dam building all have to do with their survival. The tree bark is their primary food source and the beavers have to get to it before predators get to them. So they build a dam that forms a pond. Then they can build their lodge, or den, in the pond, which serves as a protective mote. And if you think beaver dams are engineering marvels, consider their lodges.

The lodge, like the dam, is the product of a lot of chewing, dragging, piling, and mud packing. But unlike the dam's wall-like function, the lodge is a multi-

chambered design that's constructed from the inside out by lots of nibbling. This dome-shaped structure can be up to six feet high and several feet in diameter. It has an opening at the top for ventilation, and once it freezes, it's as solid as a keep, accessible only from underwater tunnels. These portals lead up through multiple levels, with rooms appointed for specific activities: storage, eating, sleeping. The lodge can hold several beaver generations and does, since beavers mate for life and allow their kits to stay with them for two years to help with raising younger siblings.

The lodges are so snug and cozy that there's no

need for the animals to hibernate—the interior will stay above freezing even if temperatures dip to the single digits.

Beavers, like otters and other mamals sought out for their sumptuous pelts, teetered on the brink of extinction. In fact, they darn well fell off the brink in England where they've been extinct since the thirteenth century thanks to an insatiable fur trade. In North America, the Hudson Bay Company's pursuit of beaver fur was largely responsible for foraging into the Pacific Northwest and establishing settlements in Canada.

Beavers are controversial critters because of their dam building and pond making. Towns on the North Shore don't need any boost to increase their odds of floods. But most conservationists agree that the ponds stimulate habitat growth by attracting a diversity of wildlife.

Rowley Marsh

A slow and steady snow has been falling all morning and could continue into the night. It has settled on the Rowley Marsh like an insistent fog bank with strands of defiant brown grass sticking up here and there along the water's edge. The snowy sky is a luminous shade of pewter. A red fox suddenly appears out of nowhere. The tonal composition of the landscape is so perfect it would make Whistler weep.

Foxes have a way of making every scene they appear in more complete, more charged with an aura of surprise and possibility. They're the smallest of the North American dogs and like the coyote, have an undeserved and unflattering reputation because they're smart, clever, and may have been caught with their snouts in a chicken coop more than a few times.

Foxes are omnivores and rely more on scavenging than on their hunting skills. They eat mice and squirrels as well as fruit, berries, and beetles.

They mate in mid-winter and are attentive parents to their litter of two to four kits. The male is solicitous of the vixen, bringing her food for the first few weeks while she's nursing the kits. When they're weaned at about two months, the kits will leave the den under their parents' sharp eyes and learn how to hunt for themselves. The family stays together until autumn, when they all go their separate ways until the mating season starts again in the winter.

The red fox will go to great lengths to avoid leaving its scent—hopping fences, choosing a water route through a stream, leaving its urine mark in scattered places to confuse its predator. Still, despite its cunning and wiliness, fox don't fare well in the wild and their

life expectancy is sadly brief, only four to five years. Predation and competition for resources are the main cause.

This fox in the Rowley Marsh might do better as long as the winter isn't too harsh and he avoids crossing paths with his nemesis, the coyote. As he gracefully lopes along the water's edge, the white tip of his tail is outlined against the backdrop of grey-blue water and his copper-red body is resplendent against the snow's whiteness. A winter tableau made more enchanting by the fox's presence.

Bald Hill West, Middleton

Most New Englanders might agree that the best thing about February is its length. Stuffed between winter's gala festivities and spring's exuberent promise, February lacks the jollity of one and the zest of the other. But it *is* short. And on the plus side, daylight is noticeably

longer, and with the next full moon, spring will be underway. Here at the Bald Hill Reservation, delicate snowdrops that someone planted have optimistically pushed up through the cold earth, so crocuses couldn't be too far behind. Other life forms aren't entirely convinced. Newts, salamanders, trout, frogs, and turtles continue their winter break under logs, leaves and mud near the pond.

And then there are otters.

Following their tracks that lead to Pout Pond puts the fun into February. Otters are a hoot. They're the class clowns of the waterways, the obliging nuts who would don balloon hats if they were offered.

Northern river otters on the east coast and sea otters on the west are, like fishers, members of the Mustelidae family that includes weasels, minks, martens, and the like. They're solidly built and up to four and half feet long including their tails, which make up a third of the total body length. Their webbed hind feet and sleek body shape make them agile, no, downright gymnastic swimmers,

and their ability to seal off nostrils and close ear holes lets them gleefully whip around underwater for a good four minutes.

Otters are chatty, outrageously sociable creatures that love to play, catch fish, play, groom their thick, silky fur to keep it water resistant, catch mice, and . . . play.

They make their dens on river and pond banks and spend much of their time swimming and goofing around. Sliding headfirst down a snowy slope on their tummies is a favorite activity, getting them through the February doldrums, no doubt.

These winsome mammals were looking down the long barrel of extinction about a hundred years ago, due to zealous trapping practices for their sumptuous fur. In 1911, world governments tried to put a stop to the sea otter hunting frenzy by instituting laws to protect them. This has helped somewhat and their numbers are inching back up. Good news for the playful everywhere.

Chapter 15

Early Spring
Nahant Thicket

Spring is amazing. It's a wonder that is repeated and repeated, well, every spring. There are some years in New England when everyone is absolutely certain that it's just not going to happen after such a ferociously bleak and interminably long winter. But it always does.

A friend who has a house facing the Atlantic Ocean here in Nahant remembers past winters when nor'easter storms left hunks of seaweed splattered menacingly on her second-story bedroom window. There was also a winter when a sinkhole the size of a truck appeared in her backyard overnight. But spring came. The rains stopped. The sun shone. The hole was fixed.

In a few weeks, this thicket will be ablaze with the new leaves of red maples. Snow fleas are already active and scurrying around at the base of their trunks. Colorful lichens emerge with a brilliant intensity that defies the rest of the drab, muted landscape, not yet in bloom.

On a nearby hillside, buried under several feet of loose earth, rocks, and dead leaves, a coiled throng of garter snakes begins to stir. These are the most common snakes in New England and can be found anywhere from craggy rocks to open fields or dank cellars. Garter snakes gather together in a hibernaculum deep underground during the cold winter months, and they are among the first animals to respond to spring's warming signals. Early spring is also mating time for the viviparous, or live-bearing, snakes, which will produce a litter of up to fifty baby garters by mid-August.

Off the coast of Salem's Misery Island wood ducks and hooded mergansers dive and bob offshore as they migrate north in anticipation of summer, and at the

Marblehead Wildlife Sanctuary the return of a variety of warblers has birdwatchers so excited they can hardly stand still.

More evidence of spring can be seen while kayaking in Ipswich. Apple-green tufts of spartina grass outline a hedge of new stubble along the marshes' muddy banks. Schools of alewives, plankton filtering members of the herring family, dart through warming waters on their way to spawning grounds in nearby rivers.

Vernal pools are warming up and soon the first "peep-peep!" of a spring peeper will break through the monotony of night's stillness to announce that life is beginning to stir. The earth is once again tilting just so and light spills like warm honey over this remarkably diverse landscape of Essex County, all in a gleeful celebration of spring.

Bibliography

Coastal Geology and Beach Formation

Ammen, Daniel. *The Atlantic Coast.* New York: Scribner, 1883.

Colvert, Edwin, editorial consultant. *Our Continent: A Natural History of North America.* Washington, D.C.: National Geographic Society, 1976.

Dennen, W. H. *The Rocks of Cape Ann.* Rockport, Mass.: W. H. Dennen, 2001.

Duncan, Roger F., and John P. Ware. *A Cruising Guide to the New England Coast: Including the Hudson River, Long Island Sound, and the Coast of New Brunswick.* New York: Putnam & Sons, 1990.

Hay, John, and Peter Farb. *The Atlantic Shore: Human and Natural History from Long Island to Labrador.* E. Orleans, Mass.: Parnassus Imprints, 1996.

Hirsch, Ron. *Save Our Oceans and Coasts.* New York: Delacorte Press, 1993.

Hooper, Rosanne. *Life on the Coastlines.* Chicago: World Book, 2001.

Jorgensen, Neil. *A Guide to New England's Landscape.* Barre, Mass.: Barre Publishers, 1971.

Kaufman, Wallace, and Orrin H. Pilkey, Jr. *The Beaches Are Moving: The Drowning of America's Shoreline.* Garden City, N.Y.: Anchor Press, 1979.

Lamb, Simon, and David Sington. *Earth Story.* Princeton, N.J.: Princeton University Press, 1998.

Massachusetts Office of Coastal Zone Management. *Massachusetts Coast Guide to Boston and the North Shore.* Boston: Massachusetts Office of Coastal Zone Management, 2004.

May, Julian. *The Land Beneath the Sea.* New York: Holliday House, 1971.

Oldale, Robert N. *Cape Cod and the Islands: The Geologic Story.* E. Orleans, Mass.: Parnassus Imprints, 1992.

Pilkey, Orrin H. *A Celebration of the World's Barrier Islands.* New York: Columbia University Press, 2003.

Raymo, Chet, and Maureen E. Raymo. *Written in Stone: A Geological History of the Northeastern United States.* Hensonville, N.Y.: Black Dome Press, 1989, 2001.

Skehan, James W. *Roadside Geology of Massachusetts.* Missoula: Mountain Press Publishing, 2001.

Waters, John F. *Exploring New England Shores: A Beachcomber's Handbook.* Lexington, Mass.: Stone Wall, 1974.

White, Laurence B. *Life in the Shifting Dunes: A Popular Field Guide to the Natural History of Castle Neck, Ipswich, Massachusetts.* Boston: Museum of Science, 1960.

Archaeology and Paleoindian History

Aloian, Molly, and Bobbie Kalman. *Nations of the Northeast Coast.* New York: Crabtree, 2006.

Bonfanti, Leo. *Biographies and Legends of the New England Indians,* volume 1. Danvers, Mass.: Old Salt Box Publishing, 1993.

_____. *Biographies and Legends of the New England Indians,* volume 2. Burlington, Mass.: Pride Publications, 1970.

Bourque, Bruce J., with Steven L. Cox and Ruth H. Whitehead. *Twelve Thousand Years: American Indians in*

Maine. Lincoln: University of Nebraska Press, 2001.

Fetchko, Peter, John Grimes, and William Phippen. *Stone Age New England: 10,000 Years of History: An Exhibit at the Peabody Museum of Salem, October 1, 1975 through May 1, 1976.* Salem, Mass.: The Museum, 1976.

Lemonick, Michael D., and Andrea Dorfman. "Who Were the First Americans?" *Time Magazine*, March 13, 2006.

Sattler, Hellen Roney. *The Earliest Americans.* New York: Clarion, 1993.

Snow, Dean R. *The Archaeology of New England.* New York: Academic Press, 1980.

Waugh, Elizabeth. *The First People of Cape Ann: Native Americans on the North Coast of Massachusetts Bay.* Gloucester, Mass.: Dogtown Books, 2005.

Wingate, Phillippa, and Struan Reid. *Who Were the First North Americans?* Tulsa: EDC Publishing, 2003.

Social and Political History

Gertsch, Karin M. *Cape Ann and Vicinity: A Guide for Residents and Visitors.* Essex, Mass.: Acorn Press, 1997.

Hale, Richard W., Jr. *Along the Coast of Essex County.* Boston: Junior League of Boston, 1984.

Sargent, William. *The House on Ipswich Marsh.* Hanover, N.H.: University Press of New England, 2005.

Thomson, Betty Flanders. *The Changing Face of New England.* New York: Macmillan, 1958.

Tree, Christina. *How New England Happened: A Guide to New England through its History.* Boston: Little, Brown, 1976.

Mammals

Beaver

Kelsey, Elin. *Beavers.* Toronto: Grollier, 1985.

Lane, Margaret. *The Beaver.* New York: Dial Press, 1981.

Roels, Lliane. *The Beaver.* New York: Grosset & Dunlap, 1969.

Tresselt, Alvin. *The Beaver Pond.* New York: Lothrop, Lee & Shepard, 1970.

Turner, Matt. *Beavers.* Chicago: Raintree, 2004.

Coyotes

Barrett, Jalma. *Coyote.* Woodbridge, Conn.: Blackbirch Press, 2000.

Greenland, Caroline. *Coyote.* Toronto: Grollier, 1986.

Lepthien, Emilie U. *Coyotes.* Chicago: Childrens Press, 1993.

Mattern, Joanne. *The Coyote.* Mankato, Minn.: Capstone High/Low Books, 1999.

Swanson, Diane. *Coyotes.* Milwaukee: Gareth Stevens Publishing, 2002.

Marine Mammals

Davidson, Susannah. *Whales and Dolphins.* Tulsa: EDC Publishing, 2003.

Hoke, Helen, and Valerie Pitt. *Whales.* New York: Watts, 1981.

Macmillan, Dianne M. *Humpback Whales.* Minneapolis: Caroirhoda Books, 2004.

Papastavrou, Vassili. *Whale.* New York: Knopf; distributed by Random House, 1993.

White-tailed Deer

Bailey, Jill. *Discovering Deer.* New York: Bookwright Press, 1988.

Patent, Dorothy Hinshaw. *White-tailed Deer.* Minneapolis: Lemur Publishing, 2005.

Rue, Leonard Lee. *The World of the White-tailed Deer.* Philadelphia: Lippincott, 1962.

Other Mammals

Ahlstrom, Mark E. *The Foxes.* Mankato, Minn.: Crestwood House, 1983.

Brownell, Barbara M. *Amazing Otters.* Washington, D.C.: National Geographic Society, 1989.

Dingwall, Laima. *Opossum.* Toronto: Grollier, 1985.

Everett, Eileen. *Foxes.* Windemere, Fla.: Rourke Publications, 1981.

Giles, Bridget. *Sea Otters.* Danbury, Conn.: Grollier Educational, 2001.

Mizumura, Kazue. *The Opossum.* New York: Crowell, 1974.

Porter, Keith, and Wendy Meadway. *Discovering Rabbits and Hares.* New York: Bookwright Press, 1988.

Pringle, Laurence P. *Follow a Fisher.* New York: Crowell, 1973.

Roach, Marilynne K. *Dune Fox.* Boston: Little, Brown, 1977.

Animal Behavior

Bancroft, Henrietta, and Richard G. Van Gelder. *Animals in Winter.* New York: Harper Collins, 1997.

Barker, Will. *Winter-Sleeping Wildlife.* New York: Harper, 1958.

Heinrich, Bernd. *Winter World: The Ingenuity of Animal Survival.* New York: Harper Collins, 2003.

Malcolm, Penny. *Animal Migration.* New York: Bookwright, 1987.

Marchand, Peter J. *Life in the Cold: An Introduction to Winter Ecology.* Hanover, N.H.: University Press of New England, 1987.

McClung, Robert M. *Animals that Build Their Homes.* Washington, D.C.: National Geographic Society, 1976.

Stokes, Donald. *A Guide to Nature in Winter.* Boston: Little, Brown, 1976.

Tison, Annette, and Talus Taylor. *Amazing Animal Builders.* New York: Grosset & Dunlap, 1989.

Birds

Bull, John, and John Farrand, Jr. *National Audubon Society Field Guide to North American Birds: Eastern Region.* New York: Alfred A. Knopf, 1994.

Darling, Louis. *The Gull's Way.* New York: Morrow, 1965.

Gans, Roma. *How Do Birds Find Their Way?* New York: Harper Collins, 1996.

Ivy, Bill. *Gulls.* Toronto: Grolier, 1987.

Mallet, Sandy. *A Year with New England's Birds: A Guide to Twenty-Five Field Trips.* Somersworth, N.H.: New Hampshire Publishing, 1978.

Reynolds, John. *Birds of Prey.* Sussex, England: Wayland, 1974.

Ross, Judy Thompson. *Canada Goose.* Toronto: Grollier, 1985.

Russell, Franklin. *Hawk in the Sky.* New York: Holt, Rinehart & Winston, 1965.

Sparks, John. *Bird Behavior.* New York: Grosset & Dunlap, 1970.

Stokes, Donald, and Lillian Stokes. A *Guide to Bird Behavior,* volume 2. Boston: Little, Brown, 1983.

Webb, Sophie. *Looking for Seabirds: Journal from an Alaskan Voyage.* Boston: Houghton Mifflin, 2004.

Wetmore, Alexander. *Song and Garden Birds of North America.* Washington, D.C.: National Geographic Society, 1975.

Marshes and Wetlands

Beatty, Richard. *Wetlands.* Austin: Raintree Steck-Vaughn, 2002.

Carroll, David M. *Swampwalker's Journal: A Wetlands Year.* Boston: Houghton Mifflin, 1999.

Fleisher, Paul. *Salt Marsh.* New York: Benchmark Books, 1999.

Gates, David Alan. *Seasons of the Salt Marsh.* Old Greenwich, Conn.: Chatham Press, 1975.

Sargent, William. *Shallow Waters: A Year on Cape Cod's Pleasant Bay.* Boston: Houghton Mifflin, 1981.

Sterling, Dorothy. *The Outer Lands: A Natural History Guide to Cape Cod, Martha's Vineyard, Nantucket, Block Island and Long Island.* New York: W.W. Norton, 1978.

Wallace, Marianne D. *America's Wetlands: Guide to Plants and Animals.* Golden, Colo.: Fulcrum Publishing, 2004.

Watson, Galadriel. *Wetlands.* New York: Weigl Publishers, 2006.

Ponds and Vernal Pools

Caduto, Michael J. *Pond and Brook: A Guide to Nature in Freshwater Environments.* Hanover, N.H.: University Press of New England, 1990.

Kenney, Leo P., and Matthew R. Burne. *A Field Guide to the Animals of Vernal Pools.* Westborough: Massachusetts Division of Fisheries & Wildlife, Natural Heritage & Endangered Species Program: Vernal Pool Association, 2000.

Walker, Sally M. *Fireflies.* Minneapolis: Lerner Publications, 2001.

Marine Animals and Environment

Allen, Thomas B., Bob Devine, and Donald Dale Jackson. *Treasures of the Tide.* Washington, D.C.: NWF Books, 1990.

Amos, William H. *The Life of the Seashore.* New York: Mc-Graw Hill, 1966.

Doris, Ellen. *Marine Biology: Ocean Shores and Coastal Waters.* New York: Thames and Hudson, 1993.

Fleisher, Paul. *Tide Pool.* New York: Benchmark Books, 1998.

Giambarba, Paul. *What Is It . . . At the Beach?* Barre, Mass.: Scrimshaw Press; distributed by Barre Publishers, 1969.

Hooper, Rosanne. *Life on the Coastlines.* Chicago: World Book, 2001.

Johnson, Sylvia A. *Crabs.* Minneapolis: Lerner Publications, 1982.

Kite, L. Patricia. *Down in the Sea: The Jellyfish.* Morton Grove, Ill.: A. Whitman, 1992.

Lerman, Matthew. *Marine Biology: Environment, Diversity and Ecology.* Menlo Park, Calif.: Benjamin Cummings Publishing, 1986.

Martinez, Andrew J. *Marine Life of the North Atlantic: Canada to New England.* Locust Valley, N.Y.: Aqua Quest Publications, 2003.

Silver, Donald M. *One Small Square: Seashore.* New York: Scientific American Books for Young Readers, 1993.

Silverstein, Alvin, and Virginia Silverstein. *Life in a Tidal Pool.* Boston: Little, Brown, 1990.

White, Laurence B. *Life in the Shifting Dunes: A Popular Field Guide to the Natural History of Castle Neck, Ipswich, Massachusetts.* Boston: Museum of Science, 1960.

Whitehead, Donald W. *Diving Cape Ann and Boston's North Shore: The Complete Guide to Skin and Scuba*

Diving in Massachusetts's Undersea Paradise! Salem,
Mass.: Liquid Space Publishing, 2005.

Flora

Brown, Lauren. *Grasses, An Identification Guide.* Boston:
Houghton Mifflin, 1979.

Newcomb, Lawrence. *Newcomb's Wildflower Guide: An In-
genious New Key System for Quick, Positive Field Identification of the Wildflowers, Flowering Shrubs and Vines of
Northeastern and North Central North America.* Boston:
Little, Brown, 1977.

Treat, Rose. *The Seaweed Book: How to Find and Have Fun
with Seaweed.* New York: Star Bright Books, 1995.

Field Guides and Seasonal Guides

Alden, Peter, and Brian Cassie. *National Audubon Society
Field Guide to New England.* New York: Alfred A.
Knopf, 1998.

Berrill, Michael, and Deborah Berrill. *A Sierra Club Natu-
ralists' Guide to the North Atlantic Coast: Cape Cod to
Newfoundland.* San Francisco: Sierra Club Books, 1981.

Chartrand, Mark R. *National Audubon Society Field Guide
to the Night Sky.* New York: Alfred A. Knopf, 1991.

Estrin, Nona Bell, and Charles W. Johnson. *In Season: A
Natural History of the New England Year.* Hanover,
N.H.: University Press of New England, 2002.

Farndon, John. *Wildlife Atlas: A Complete Guide to Animals and Their Habitats.* New York: Readers Digest Association, 2002.

Jordan, E. L. *Hammond's Nature Atlas of America.* Garden
City, N.Y.: Doubleday, 1952.

Jorgensen, Neil. *A Guide to New England's Landscape.*
Barre, Mass.: Barre Publishers, 1971.

Lang, Tom. *New England Nature Watch: A Month-by-Month Guide to the Natural World Around Us.* Beverly, Mass.: Commonwealth Editions, 2003.

Lawrence, Gayle. *A Field Guide to the Familiar: Learning to Observe the Natural World.* Hanover, N.H.: University Press of New England, 1998.

Mitchell, John, and the Massachusetts Audubon Society. *The Curious Naturalist.* Englewood Cliffs, N.J.: Prentice-Hall, 1980,

Montgomery, Sy. *The Curious Naturalist: Seasons of the Wild; A Year of Nature's Magic and Mysteries.* Shelburne, Vt., 1995.

————. *The Wild Out Your Window: Exploring Nature Near at Hand.* Camden, Maine: Down East Books, 2002.

Parker, Steve. *Eyewitness: Natural World.* London: Doris Kinderslay; distributed by Houghton Mifflin, 1994.

Rezendes, Paul. *Tracking and the Art of Seeing: How to Read Animal Tracks and Signs.* New York: Harper Collins, 1999.

Spence, Pam. *The Universe.* New York: Harper Collins, 2005.

Stokes, Donald W. *A Guide to Nature in Winter: Northeast and North Central North America.* Boston: Little, Brown, 1976.

Tanner, Ogden. *New England Wilds.* New York: Time-Life Books, 1974.

Weidensaul, Scott. *Seasonal Guide to the Natural Year: A Month-by-Month Guide to Natural Events, New England and New York.* Golden, Colo.: Fulcrum Publishing, 1993.

Wernert, Susan J., consulting editor. *Readers Digest North

American Wildlife: An Illustrated Guide to 2000 Plants and Animals. New York: Readers Digest Association, 1982.

Wonder

Hay, John. *A Beginner's Faith in Things Unseen.* Boston: Beacon Press, 1994.

Index

Quascacunquen, 60

Radiocarbon dating, 17
Red foxes, 96–98
Red-tailed hawks, 87–88
Red-winged blackbirds, 31–32
Revere, 35
Rockport, xvii, 1, 37, 39
Rocks, 35
Rodinia, 1, 2, 3, 4–5
Rowley, 59
Ruminant, 27

Salem, 104
Salicornia, 57
Salisbury, 35, 38
Sand, 35
Sand dunes, 37–38
Sea level, 8
Seaweeds, 69
Sedges, 12, 27
Sharks, 7
Siasconset, 37
Spartina alterniflora, 56
Spartina patens, 57
Spermataphores, 23
Spotted salamanders, 23–24
Stellwagen, Henry, 78

Stellwagen Bank, 12, 36, 47, 74,
   75, 77, 79
Stellwagen Bank National Marine
   Sanctuary, 75
Supercontinents, 1, 4–5
Suspect terranes, 3
Swampscott, 7

Terminal moraines, 56, 57
Till, 9
Tilles Bank, 75
Tooth, 7
Topsfield, 85
Trilobites, 30
Tsunamis, 2
Tundra, 12, 16

Upwelling, 78

Vermont, 19
Vernal pools, 22
Volcanoes, 2

Weather, 12
Wingaersheek, 36
Winthrop, John, 89
Wisconsin Ice Age, 39
Wooly mammoth, 7, 12, 16, 77

DATE DUE

GAYLORD   PRINTED IN U.S.A.